Lev Vygotsky

Volumes of the *Continuum Library of Educational Thought* include:

St Thomas Aquinas	Vivian Boland OP
Pierre Bourdieu	Michael James Grenfell
Jerome Bruner	David Olson
John Dewey	Richard Pring
John Holt	Roland Meighan
John Locke	Alexander Moseley
Maria Montessori	Marion O'Donnell
John Henry Newman	James Arthur and Guy Nicholls
Plato	Robin Barrow
Lev Vygotsky	René van der Veer
Rudolf Steiner	Heiner Ullrich
Jean Piaget	Richard Kohler
Jean-Jacques Rousseau	Jürgen Oelkers
E.G. West	James Tooley
Mary Wollstonecraft	Susan Laird

See www.continuumbooks.com for further details.

Also available from Continuum:

Philosophy of Education, Richard Pring

Greatest Educators Ever, Frank M. Flanagan

Lev Vygotsky

RENÉ VAN DER VEER

Continuum Library of Educational Thought
Series Editor: Richard Bailey
Volume 10

Continuum International Publishing Group
The Tower Building   80 Maiden Lane
11 York Road   Suite 704
London SE1 7NX   New York NY 10038

www.continuumbooks.com

© René van der Veer 2007

First published 2007
Reprinted 2011

All rights reserved. No part of this publication may be reproduced or transmitted in any form or by any means, electronic or mechanical, including photocopying, recording, or any information storage or retrieval system, without prior permission in writing from the publishers.

René van der Veer has asserted his right under the Copyright, Designs and Patents Act, 1988, to be identified as Author of this work.

British Library Cataloguing-in-Publication Data
A catalogue record for this book is available from the British Library.

ISBN: 978-0-8264-8409-3 (hardcover)

Library of Congress Cataloguing-in-Publication Data
Veer, René van der, 1952–
Lev Vygotsky / René van der Veer.
   p. cm. – (Continuum library of educational thought)
Includes bibliographical references and index.
ISBN-13: 978-0-8264-8409-3 (hardcover)
ISBN-10: 0-8264-8409-3 (hardcover)
1. Vygotskii, L. S. (Lev Semenovich), 1896–1934.   2. Educational psychology.
3. Developmental psychology.   I. Title.   II. Series.

LB1051.V44 2007
370.15–dc22
2007018517

Typeset by Aptara Books Ltd.

Contents

Foreword	vii
Series Editor's Preface	x
Preface	xii
Introduction	1
Part 1 Intellectual Biography	11
1 Lev Vygotsky	13
Notes to Part 1	29
Part 2 Critical Exposition of Vygotsky's Work	33
2 Early Writings	35
3 Creating Cultural-historical Theory	48
4 The Zone of Proximal Development	75
5 Cross-cultural Education	97
Notes to Part 2	106
Part 3 The Reception, Influence and Relevance of Vygotsky's Work Today	111
6 Contemporary Educational Research	113
7 Conclusions	136
Notes to Part 3	140
Bibliography	143
Name Index	161
Subject Index	165

Foreword

Whether he was a natural product or an artifact of twentieth-century Russian-Soviet psychology, Lev Vygotsky undoubtedly affected the landscape of modern psychology. In *Vygotsky's Educational Thinking*, René van der Veer examines the intellectual and affective roots of Vygotsky as a thinker, delineating for the reader his interpretation of Vygotsky as both the man and anti-man of his time, and sketching Vygotsky's profound contribution to psychology.

As Van der Veer suggests, historians of science might '... never be able to fully explain' (p. 4) the popularity of Vygotsky's ideas in the West. And this very inexplicability is, at least in part, what is so attractive about Vygotsky's writings. Like any unsolved mystery, Vygotsky's creativity has attracted many Western and Russian researchers.

In his new volume, Van der Veer's chronological, vertical perspective starts with Vygotsky's biography (Chapter 1), explores his early writings (which are less known to the West) (Chapter 2), investigates the roots of Vygotsky's cultural-historical theory (Chapter 3), pays particular attention to the concept of the zone of proximal development (Chapter 4), presents Vygotsky's ideas on cultural psychology (Chapter 5), and ends with a summary of Vygotsky's impact on modern psychology (Chapter 6). The book focuses primarily on Vygotsky's contributions to education, but the author extensively covers a number of general topics in Vygotsky's writing (e.g. the concepts of cultural tool and higher mental function), providing an overview of Vygotsky's work in general. Van der Veer's book is a valuable account of Vygotsky's work and will be helpful not only to historians of psychology and education, but also to students, researchers and practitioners in both fields.

As Vygotsky was a major figure in Russian academic history, this is not the first book to profile him. Russian authors such as

Андрей Брущлинский [Andrey Brushlinsky], Александр Эткинд [Aleksandr Etkind], Валерий Петухов [Valery Petukhov], Андрей Пузырей [Andrey Puzyrey], Ирина Сироткина [Irina Sirotkina], Владимир Умрихин [Vladimir Umrikhin] and Михаил Ярощевский [Mikhail Yaroshevsky], among others, have all offered accounts of Vygotsky. Their accounts, although different from each other, offer a more horizontal perspective, representing Vygotsky's creativity as a part of the 'shared consciousness', 'the Russian thought' of the early twentieth century. These authors, however, wrote primarily in Russian, which makes their writings rather inaccessible to psychologists and educators of the West. This is why Van der Veer's volume is especially important – it connects Russian and Western views of Vygotsky's creativity.

As is the case with any historical figure, different accounts of Vygotsky's life present some discrepancies in details, but how important are such minor details? Such discrepancies are only indications of how complex the reality in which we live is – the whole country witnessed 70-plus years of socialism in the former USSR, and there is still no uniform interpretation of what happened, why it happened, why it lasted as long as it did, and most importantly, what lessons should be learned from those years. Yet, there are some common features that unify all of Vygotsky's students. Here are three selected ones.

First, readers of Vygotsky agree on his inspired and inspiring view of a human being as a creator and modifier of knowledge. For Vygotsky, a child is not a mechanical structure that acts as prescribed by some program while moving through the stages of development. Rather, the child is an active 'creator' of her higher mental functions, because each and every one of them needs to be constructed from innate building blocks with mental tools and cultural guidelines suggested by adults. This act of construction is human in its essence and unique for every child. This humanistic interpretation of development where due respect is paid to both nature and nurture, with the former being 'the material' and the latter being 'the guidelines', insists on the magic of a merge and unification of the two occurring in each individual child inimitably. Vygotsky applauds each and every child, whether typically developing or not, for his or her construction of a distinctive self.

Second, there is a consensus on the breadth of Vygotsky's creativity and his contribution to many subfields of psychology and human thought. Any book on Vygotsky is necessarily limited, simply because he wrote thousands of printed pages on different subjects. What is also important to note is the heterogeneity, both chronological and concurrent, of Vygotsky as a thinker. His writings are contradictory in places, and his self-reflections on a 'crisis in psychology' capture his internal tension and the tension in the field, implying the inevitability and absolute necessity of this tension for the development of psychology as a field. Psychology was in crisis before Vygotsky, during Vygotsky, after Vygotsky, and for the foreseeable future. For Vygotsky, when the crisis is over, psychology as a science is dead.

Third, Vygotsky's creativity is not characterized by a large body of empirical research, but rather by brilliant experimental ideas. Although Vygotsky did not have the chance to implement and evaluate his own ideas, others have and still do. What is specific to Vygotsky's writings is this flavor of richness of testable hypotheses. He generated many ideas and tested very few. That is why reading Vygotsky is productive; one always walks away with a thing or two to try.

Thus, there will always be followers of Vygotsky, and Van der Veer's account of the man and his ideas will serve them well. In essence, Van der Veer does to Vygotsky's creativity what Vygotsky himself did to Shakespeare's *Hamlet* – he drew 'the reader's attention to one possible and admittedly subjective interpretation' of the work 'while preserving its mysterious character' (see p. 37 of current volume).

Elena L. Grigorenko
Yale University, USA
Moscow State University, Russia

Series Editor's Preface

Education is sometimes presented as an essentially practical activity. It is, it seems, about teaching and learning, curriculum and what goes on in schools. It is about achieving certain ends, using certain methods, and these ends and methods are often prescribed for teachers, whose duty it is to deliver them with vigour and fidelity. With such a clear purpose, what is the value of theory?

Recent years have seen politicians and policy-makers in different countries explicitly denying *any* value or need for educational theory. A clue to why this might be is offered by a remarkable comment by a British Secretary of State for Education in the 1990s: 'having any ideas about how children learn, or develop, or feel, should be seen as subversive activity'. This pithy phrase captures the problem with theory: it subverts, challenges and undermines the very assumptions on which the practice of education is based.

Educational theorists, then, are trouble-makers in the realm of ideas. They pose a threat to the *status quo* and lead us to question the common sense presumptions of educational practices. But this is precisely what they should do because the seemingly simple language of schools and schooling hides numerous contestable concepts that in their different usages reflect fundamental disagreements about the aims, values and activities of education.

Implicit within the *Continuum Library of Educational Thought* is an assertion that theories and theorizing are vitally important for education. By gathering together the ideas of some of the most influential, important and interesting educational thinkers, from the Ancient Greeks to contemporary scholars, the series has the ambitious task of providing an accessible yet authoritative resource for a generation of students and practitioners. Volumes within the series are written by acknowledged leaders in the field, who were selected both for their scholarship and their ability to make often complex ideas accessible to a diverse audience.

It will always be possible to question the list of key thinkers that are represented in this series. Some may question the inclusion of certain thinkers; some may disagree with the exclusion of others. That is inevitably going to be the case. There is no suggestion that the list of thinkers represented within the *Continuum Library of Educational Thought* is in any way definitive. What is incontestable is that these thinkers have fascinating ideas about education, and that taken together, the *Library* can act as a powerful source of information and inspiration for those committed to the study of education.

Richard Bailey
Roehampton University, London

Preface

In writing this book I have made extensive use of earlier books and articles published by Jaan Valsiner and myself. Over the years we have been cooperating so much on cultural-historical theory and other topics that it is sometimes difficult to say where he ends and I commence. Therefore, I would like to thank both of us for our helpful suggestions, valuable insights and critical comments. I also owe thanks to David Allen for his useful information on Stanislavsky. Paul Vedder and Seth Chaiklin gave critical comments on parts of the manuscript which I unsuccessfully tried to ignore. Thanks for that as well. The mistakes that remain are mine, of course. The problem is that Vygotsky addressed so many topics with so many repercussions for our science that it would need another Vygotsky to discuss them adequately from the viewpoint of present-day science. Which I am not. Fortunately, the readers will bring their own expertise to this book and will fill in the details I left out and correct any errors I made. What results of this joint effort will hopefully be a stimulating overview of Vygotsky's views on education.

René van der Veer
Leiden, July 2006

Introduction

In July 1925 a certain Dr Leo Vygotsky presented a talk at the International Conference on the Education of the Deaf in London.[1] The approximately 450 attendants were mostly teachers from schools for the deaf with no academic background. Vygotsky argued that social isolation is the greatest danger for deaf children and that they should be taught vocal speech from an early age. Their education should take place at labor schools, where they are not separated from normal social life (Vygotsky 1925; cf. Brill 1984). I know of no Western publication that ever referred to the written version of Vygotsky's talk.

In the late 1920s and early 1930s the *Pedagogical Seminary and Journal of Genetic Psychology*, edited by G. Stanley Hall, published a short series of three articles by three unknown Soviet psychologists describing what they called 'the cultural development of the child' (Leontiev 1932; Luria 1928b; Vygotsky 1929). The series was followed by two brief accounts of a psychological expedition to Central Asia destined to investigate this so-called cultural development and written by one of its participants, Alexander Luria (Luria 1932a; 1934). To the best of my knowledge, none of their Western contemporaries ever referred to these articles in writing.

At approximately the same time the German Marxist journal *Unter dem Banner des Marxismus* published an article on the genetic roots of thinking and speech by a certain Wygotski (1929). It was read by the literary critic and philosopher Walter Benjamin who commented that it was Vygotsky's 'merit to have demonstrated the meaning of the chimpanzee research for the fundamentals of linguistics' (Benjamin 1935/1972, p. 472). He also praised Vygotsky for his discovery that egocentric speech is the precursor of thought (ibid., p. 475). I know of no other writer who ever referred to Vygotsky's German article.

Vygotsky's and Luria's (1930a) joint paper on egocentric speech, presented by Luria at the ninth International Congress of Psychology in New Haven in 1929 and summarized in the proceedings, left no other trace in the printed records. Nor did it cause a stir among Western colleagues.

Several articles written in the late 1920s to acquaint the Western reader with developments in Russian psychology (Borovski 1929; Luria 1928a; Schniermann 1928) discussed first of all the well-known work of the grand old men of Russian psychology, Ivan Pavlov and Vladimir Bekhterev. In addition, attention was paid to the work of the younger generation of Basov, Blonsky and (primarily) Kornilov (cf. Van der Veer and Valsiner 1991). Vygotsky's name was only mentioned in passing and his ideas were not exposed in any way.

In 1934 the journal *Archives of Neurology and Psychiatry* published a paper by Vygotsky on a method to investigate the conceptual thinking of schizophrenics (Vygotsky 1934b). It was translated by Kasanin, who also revised Vygotsky's method into a 'Vygotsky test' (Hanfmann and Kasanin 1937; Kasanin and Hanfmann 1938) and proposed a quantitative scoring method (Hanfmann and Kasanin 1942). This test from 'the Russian psychiatrist Vygotsky' met with some initial interest, but never became part of the toolbox of Western clinicians (see Van der Veer and Valsiner 1991, pp. 278–83).

In other words, despite Vygotsky's personal contacts with such noted Western psychologists as Kurt Koffka and Kurt Lewin (cf. Van der Veer and Valsiner 1991) and despite active efforts by Luria to spread Vygotsky's ideas, to arrange translations and so on, Vygotsky left virtually no trace in Western psychology until his rediscovery. By 1945 there was hardly a Western psychologist who had ever heard of his name, let alone read one of the very few articles available in the modern languages. To have bracketed together the names of, say, Koffka, Watson, Lewin, Piaget and Vygotsky would have seemed absurd, because Vygotsky was a non-entity at the time.

The contrast with the present time could hardly be bigger. Today the work of Lev Vygotsky is well known all over the Western world. His books and papers have been translated into dozens of languages. General introductory psychology textbooks mention his name as a researcher who introduced the social perspective in psychology and books on developmental psychology contrast his views with those of Piaget. Researchers from all walks of the social sciences and the humanities feel inspired by his work and a recent inventory showed him to be among the 100 most eminent psychologists of the twentieth century (Haggbloom et al. 2002).

It is not at all easy to explain this tremendous shift in Vygotsky's popularity from the 1930s to now. A tentative and preliminary answer would have to deal with the reasons for his not becoming known in the 1930s and the reasons for his becoming popular in the latter part of the twentieth century. To explain why Vygotsky's ideas made no headway in the Western world in the 1930s one might point to several factors. First, he and his colleagues published only a handful of papers which many psychologists may have simply overlooked amidst the thousands of other publications (cf. Valsiner 1988). Second, at that time the dominant tradition of thought in psychology and education was behaviorism, whose basic tenets were impossible to reconcile with Vygotsky's approach. For example, when Vygotski (1929) published his first English article in the *Pedagogical Seminary and Journal of Genetic Psychology*, about one third of the papers dealt with the adventures of maze-running white rats. This is all the more remarkable because that journal was not exclusively devoted to experimental research. One might think, then, that Vygotsky's ideas went against the *Zeitgeist*, that his ideas were too strange to be thought at that specific time in that specific culture (Boring 1950, p. 3). At any rate, the fact is that Vygotsky's ideas fell on deaf ears in the English-speaking psychological world of the time and that his ideas only resurfaced in the 1960s (for a detailed analysis of the two waves of English publications of Vygotsky's ideas in the West, see Valsiner 1988, pp. 156–62).

In the 1960s and 1970s, Vygotsky's ideas may have gained increasing popularity because of a growing dissatisfaction with existing ideas. In its extreme form, behaviorism was now seen by many to be inadequate and cognitive psychology returned to the study of the mental processes that underlie behavior. Piaget was increasingly (and undeservedly) viewed as a theorist who pictured the learning child as a solitary being divorced from the social surroundings and institutions (Bruner 1984, p. 96) not unlike Robinson Crusoe on his island. Critical psychologists were looking for an approach that took account of the social or societal origin of human behavior. Together these factors may have created a climate that was ripe for the acceptance of Vygotsky's theories. Somewhat later, it was realized that Vygotsky's cultural-historical theory was a useful analytical tool when thinking about the problems of minorities caused by the new waves of immigration (Kozulin 2003), which may have contributed to the still wider use of Vygotsky's thinking. One may also think of relevant sociological factors contributing to Vygotsky's popularity (e.g. the fact that very visible figures such as Alexander Luria, Jerome Bruner and Michael Cole have actively promoted his work in the USA, while Andrew Sutton did the same in the UK), but in the end, I think, we will never be able to fully explain it. Perhaps the great French psychologist Pierre Janet (1928, p. 32) was right after all when he claimed that there is fashion in science just like there is fashion in dresses and hats. No historical account, I believe, whether internalist or externalist, can exhaustively explain the paradigm shifts that we witness regularly.

Meanwhile, the fact that Vygotsky became popular so long after his death causes its own problems. We have forgotten so much of the psychology of the early twentieth century that it is easy to attribute ideas to Vygotsky that did not originate with him. Or, we may fail to see the significance of the theories he advanced. No one less than Edwin Boring (1950, p. ix), in his famous *A History of Experimental Psychology*, warned against this possibility arguing that the psychologist needs historical sophistication, because 'without such knowledge he sees the present in distorted perspective, he mistakes old facts and old views for new, and he remains unable to evaluate the significance of new movements and methods'. Boring was not talking about a merely theoretical possibility. I vividly remember attending a conference where the speaker praised Vygotsky (1930/1960, p. 426) for his 'brilliant insight' that one might teach chimpanzees sign language rather than spoken language. The speaker most probably relied on my own misleading text in *Understanding Vygotsky: A Quest for Synthesis*, where I wrote that Vygotsky's suggestion 'anticipated the idea of the Gardners' experiment with Washoe by some 40 years' (Van der Veer and Valsiner 1991, p. 203). It is true that Vygotsky's suggestion anticipated the research by the Gardners and it certainly was a bright idea, but unfortunately for the speaker (and for me) it was not Vygotsky's idea. As Vygotsky (1934a, p. 83) himself noted elsewhere, the idea had been suggested by Robert Yerkes (1925, pp. 179–80; cf. Yerkes and Yerkes 1929, p. 309) several years earlier. Such examples illustrate the danger of assessing the value of a researcher's work without knowing the full historical context.

We should not forget that scientists build on the work of their predecessors and contemporaries and that their lasting success partly depends on followers. To quote Boring again:

> A simple assignment of credit occurs in spite of the fact that collateral scientists and successors have been necessary to give the new movement the importance which justifies considering it great, and in spite of the fact that a change in scientific direction occurs readily only when it moves with the *Zeitgeist* and is perhaps stifled too early for notice when the times are against it. History is a part of nature where multiple causation rules and where single effective causes are the over-simplifications, devised to bring the incomprehensible complexity of reality within the narrow compass of man's understanding. (Boring 1950, p. 744)

To reduce the number of such over-simplifications and to decrease the danger of misjudgment of the significance and originality of Vygotsky's work I have supplied some historical information in different chapters. The reader should know, however, that the historical background of Vygotsky's work and its embeddedness in the Soviet society is discussed in more detail in other sources (e.g. Van der Veer and Valsiner 1991).

Leaving aside issues of historical assessment, it can be said that the legacy of Vygotsky and his school is impressive. His so-called cultural-historical theory (outlined in Chapter 3) was influential in the creation of the new field of *cultural psychology*, the study of the culture's role in the mental life of human beings (Cole 1996; 2000). For example, researchers may investigate whether the invention of the personal computer and word-processing programs (both examples of modern cultural tools) have changed our style of writing. Or, whether becoming literate makes one better at reasoning tasks (Scribner and Cole 1981). One of the outcomes of such research is that modern psychological literature, previously largely based on data found in experiments conducted with western adolescents and assumed to be universally valid, now pays much more attention to cultural variations in behavior and cognitive processes.

Vygotsky's views on mental testing led to the new field of *dynamic assessment* (see Chapter 6). Although much needs to be done to improve the quality of research, a few preliminary conclusions can be drawn from this type of research. First, Vygotsky's hunch that a dual testing procedure may be more informative than the traditional single testing procedure seems valid. Children who score approximately the same on traditional IQ tests differ in their ability to profit from assistance. In different investigations the researchers have distinguished those who gain much from help and those who gain little. It is thought that the first group may be simply culturally deprived whereas the second group may have organic problems. There is also evidence that school results can be predicted better on the basis of the dual testing procedure than on the basis of the old static IQ test. Second, if the above proves true, the dual testing procedure may be fairer to the individual child. For example, children who are able to profit from assistance may be offered enrichment programs which may enable them to attend regular schools rather than special ones.

Vygotsky's view on the relationship between *education and mental development* has been implemented in many instructional programs and theories (Daniels 2001; Kozulin et al. 2003; Moll 1990). Vygotsky believed that instruction in elementary school leads the child to reflect on his own mental operations and to use them deliberately and efficiently. In contemporary parlance, he believed that good teaching creates metacognitive skills. Vygotsky's global ideas have inspired many researchers to develop new instructional programs. A typical approach is to introduce children to the core concepts (*scientific concepts*) and essential relationships within a knowledge domain with the help of graphs and symbols that graphically depict them. The children are then taught to use these graphs and symbols independently as cultural tools that guide their thinking process. Often, the researchers link up to Vygotsky's idea that cognitive development relies to a considerable extent on the child's interaction with more able peers and adults, and allow for extensive classroom discussions (see Chapter 6).

Vygotsky's ideas about the development and function of inner speech found its way into *psycholinguistics* (Wertsch 1985). Strange as it may sound, Vygotsky considered language (or 'speech', in his terminology) to be the most fundamental cultural tool. The original function of speech is communication between persons, but fairly soon speech begins to serve intrapersonal goals. This claim received additional support through his discussion of the phenomenon of *egocentric speech*. Jean Piaget had first described the phenomenon of children who during play speak for themselves in a way that is often not intelligible to others. Piaget hypothesized that such speech is unintelligible, because young children are unable to take the other's point of view, i.e. they are egocentric. Only gradually will children learn to replace their egocentric speech by social speech. Vygotsky criticized Piaget's contention and carried out several little experiments to refute his views. Vygotsky noted, for example, that egocentric speech is absent or greatly reduced when the child is alone or surrounded by deaf children. This suggests that egocentric speech is meant as social communication. Vygotsky observed that the incidence of egocentric speech rises when the child is confronted with unexpected problems. This suggests that egocentric speech has some function in the solution of problems. Finally, Vygotsky noticed that egocentric speech becomes *less* intelligible as children grow older. From these results Vygotsky drew the conclusion that so-called egocentric speech (1) originates in normal, communicative speech and branches off at a later stage; (2) has as its function to steer the child's behavior when the need arises; and (3) becomes less and less intelligible to the outsider until it has become proper inner speech. According to Vygotsky, then, egocentric speech is an intermediary stage between normal, communicative speech and inner speech. Like communicative speech, it is audible, and like inner speech, it serves to guide the child's thinking. Vygotsky's arguments have inspired an enormous and still growing amount of research that cannot be summarized here (cf. Lloyd and Fernyhough 1999; Zivin 1979).

Vygotsky's criticism of existing theories about the localization of mental functions in the brain (see Chapter 3) was used to create the new discipline of *psychoneurology* (cf. Luria 1973). Throughout his scientific career Vygotsky worked as a clinical psychologist with patients with mental and physical disabilities. Over the years, he and his collaborator Alexander Luria got increasingly interested in the brain organization of mental processes. To deepen their insight, both Vygotsky and Luria (being professors of psychology) began studying medicine at the Medical Faculty of the Psychoneurological Institute in Kharkov in 1931. At the time the brain was considered as a static structure, but Vygotsky came to believe that the brain is a flexible, dynamic system. It was his colleague Alexander Luria who developed this idea further. Luria and his collaborators investigated countless patients with brain lesions and devised compensatory means for patients with severe disturbances. Together they developed the new discipline of neuropsychology, of which Oliver Sacks is now one of the main proponents. Vygotsky's original ideas may have been rather global and over-simplified, but he was one of the first to see that the brain is a flexible, dynamic system that is crucially influenced by the cultural tools one masters, notably language (Luria 1973).

Vygotsky also developed an original view on the problems of disabled children (Valsiner and Van der Veer 1991) and in Russia he is still regarded as one of the major theorists of the discipline of what is called *defectology*, i.e. that branch of psychology that deals with the problems of children with physical disabilities or mental impairments.

This list of Vygotskian research could easily be made much longer, but even as it is it is impressive enough. Clearly, whether we see Vygotsky as a researcher who polished old pearls of insight to make them shine again, whether we regard him as a genius who single-handedly created a new view of human psychology, or whether we value him for the retouching and synthesizing of existing ideas, it does not make a difference for present-day psychology. Modern psychology has recognized the value of the ideas that Vygotsky discussed, has elaborated, amended and discarded them, and will never be the same again.

Note

1. In the proceedings of the conference his name was also spelled as Vigotsky and both Warsaw and Moscow were given as his place of residence.

Part 1
Intellectual Biography

Chapter 1

Lev Vygotsky

Childhood and Youth

Lev Semyonovich Vygodsky[1] was born in Tsarist Russia in the town of Orsha in 1896. In his childhood, the Vygodsky family moved to the city of Gomel which is located in between Minsk and Kiev in White Russia. Nowadays it is a rather unhealthy place to be – the catastrophe at the nearby nuclear power plant in Chernobyl in 1986 contaminated the whole area and thyroid cancer incidence, for example, is about 100 times higher than before the accident – but at the time life could still be pleasant in Gomel and its surroundings. Swimming and boating in the local river and horseback riding belonged to the young Lev Vygotsky's pastimes. Vygotsky's parents were middle-class secular Jews who played a rather prominent role in the cultural life of Gomel. His father, Semyon L'vovich Vygodsky, was a bank employee and a representative of an insurance company who finished his career as the branch manager of the Industrial Bank in Moscow. Semyon Vygodsky was socially active and, among other things, helped create the local public library. Vygotsky's mother, Cecilia Moiseyevna Vygodskaya, was a teacher by training but devoted all her time to the household and the upbringing of her eight children. It was she who seems to have largely determined the emotional and intellectual climate in the family. The reading of books and the attendance of theater performances were actively encouraged and every night parents and children would gather to drink tea, to read aloud and discuss poetry and prose, to discuss recent plays, and to talk about anything else that came up (Vygodskaya and Lifanova 1996).

These meetings and the general family atmosphere instilled a lifelong fascination for literature and theater in the young Vygotsky.

Throughout his life he would remain fascinated with poetry, prose and play. The adult Vygotsky's knowledge of the Russian and international literature was outstanding and in private conversation, during lectures and in his scientific writings Vygotsky would often quote fragments from poems, novels and plays. As an adolescent he became infatuated with Shakespeare's *Hamlet* and his wide reading of the relevant literature eventually led to his master's thesis at Shanyavsky University (see below). The problem that eventually came to fascinate him was by what means Shakespeare and his colleagues created artistic effects in the reader (see Chapter 2). While still a student, Vygotsky began writing literary reviews for various journals and during his university years he never missed an opportunity to attend the newest performances by the famous Moscow theater groups. One may wonder whether this informal literary education may not have been at least as edifying as Vygotsky's formal training. Not only did his literary interests determine the subject of his master's thesis and his doctoral dissertation, they also must have made him sensitive to the complexities of the human mind and aversive to premature reductionist endeavors in the style of Pavlov, Bekhterev and Watson.

The young Lev (Beba to his friends) – and presumably his siblings as well – received the first part of his education at home from a private tutor, a mathematician who had been expelled from the university because of his participation in the student democratic movement. This tutor, a certain Ashpiz, had the gift of asking questions that revealed the weak points in his pupils' accounts but at the same time stimulated their further thinking (Feigenberg 1996). After five years of study with the tutor, Vygotsky entered the private local Jewish gymnasium for boys to go through the last two years of the curriculum and to receive his diploma. By all accounts, he seems to have been a very bright student who excelled in every subject, from physics and mathematics to Latin and French. With his mother, Lev Vygotsky seems to have shared a gift for languages – although he avoided conversations with native speakers claiming that his foreign accent was unbearable – and he read and understood Latin, Greek, German, French, English, Hebrew, Esperanto and Yiddish (Vygodskaya and Lifanova 1996).

Being a Jew in Tsarist Russia

Above I have said that Vygotsky's parents were secular Jews and one might well ask whether this fact is of any help in understanding Vygotsky's personality or worldview and whether it was actually important to him. In my understanding, his religious-ethnic background and the way society reacted to that background was indeed important in shaping his moral and intellectual development. Here several factors must be taken into account.

First, we must realize that feelings of anti-Semitism have always been relatively strong in Russia and that they were rather often actively encouraged and sanctioned by the authorities. These feelings regularly culminated in actual *pogroms* (of the Russian verb: *gromit* = to destroy, to ransack). During Vygotsky's lifetime, his native city Gomel witnessed pogroms in 1903 and 1906 (when Vygotsky was, respectively, seven and ten years old), and it is said that his father played an active role in the Jewish defense against these attacks (Feigenberg 1996; Gilbert 1979; Kozulin 1990; Pinkus 1988). Thus, it is likely that Lev Vygotsky himself experienced or at least heard about the sad results of these pogroms.

Second, the Tsarist authorities had devised all sorts of legislations to regulate (read 'restrict') the Jewish participation in social life. For example, Jewish citizens were not allowed to live outside a certain area (called the Pale of Settlement),[2] positions as a civil servant were not open to Jews (which also excluded the possibility of being a teacher at a state school or college) and universities used quotas for Jewish students.[3]

Third, although the Vygodskys were not religious in any deep sense of the word, they held on to traditional Jewish customs. Thus, Lev Vygotsky was taught to read the *Torah* in Hebrew, he delivered a speech at his *Bar Mitsva*, and so on. Also, he grew up in a typical Jewish intellectual milieu (with its emphasis on bookish learning and intellectual debate); he had a Jewish private tutor, and attended the Jewish gymnasium. Taken together, these factors must have stimulated an interest in Jewish identity and history and they undoubtedly created sensitivity to all sorts of anti-Semitism in particular and prejudice at large. We can, at any rate, understand certain of Vygotsky's later interests and publications against this background. For example, when Vygotsky was about 15 years old, he studied the history of the Jewish people for some time with a group of friends, using the Bible and history books as their sources. Several years later, while a university student, Vygotsky began writing reviews of books and plays for Jewish journals and local newspapers. Sometimes these reviews dealt with plays presented by Jewish groups in Yiddish (Vygotsky 1923a; 1923b; 1923c). At other times Vygotsky addressed typical Jewish issues. He discussed, for example, the image of the Yid in Russian literature and pointed out the anti-Semitic traits in Andrey Belyy's astonishing novel *Peterburg* (Vygotsky 1916a; 1916b). After the October Revolution, Vygotsky (1917) published an essay in which he welcomed liberation from the oppressive power but argued that the Jewish people were not fully ready for their new freedom (cf. Valsiner and Van der Veer 2000; Van der Veer and Valsiner 1991). Much later, we find Vygotsky writing about 'peoples developing under the influence of religious prejudices, for example the Jews' (Vygotsky 1931/1983, p. 163).

Taken together, these facts suggest that Vygotsky combined an intense interest in and identification with the Jewish identity and history with a non-religious worldview. As so often happens in the case of Jews and others who suffer discrimination, the outside hostility and harassments would almost have forced him to take an interest in his ethnic background had this interest not been there in the first place. Fortunately, the early Soviet era was one of the few periods in Russian history where outspoken anti-Semitism was less palpable. However, by that time already 20 years of Vygotsky's life had passed, years in which he had witnessed and experienced various forms of discrimination that may have shaped his view of life (Van der Veer and Valsiner 1991).

Student Years

After he finished the gymnasium, Vygotsky wished to continue his education at the university. Once again, his Jewish background threatened to play a negative role. The quota for Jewish students at Moscow

University was only 3 per cent and a lottery decided who was to belong to this number. Fortunately, Vygotsky was among the lucky few. Now he had to make up his mind about his study and future profession. Given that positions in the civil service were excluded, it seemed best to prepare for one of the liberal professions. His parents wished him to become a medical doctor and for one month in 1913 Vygotsky actually studied medicine. However, he then switched to law, which offered the opportunity to become an attorney and to live outside the Pale. Presumably, neither medicine nor law were studies that held any particular attraction to Vygotsky. In practice he seems to have used his time as a student to take as many courses as possible of his own liking at both Moscow State University and the unofficial Shanyavsky University and to attend the local theaters.

Both Moscow State University and Shanyavsky University offered courses that were particularly interesting to Vygotsky. At Moscow University, he may have taken the psychologist Georgiy Chelpanov's (1862–1936) classes and he certainly attended a course by the Humboldtian scholar Gustav Shpet (1897–1937) (see below). At Shanyavsky University, Vygotsky attended the classes given by Chelpanov's student, Pavel Blonsky (1884–1941), who would later become one of the leading figures in the creation of a Marxist psychology. The fact that Vygotsky took these courses suggests that his interest in the study of law or medicine was minimal or, at least, that his interests were much wider. His literary fascination seems to have led him to the psychology of art and creativity and, finally, to psychology in general. However, the full switch to psychology would take place somewhat later, after Vygotsky's university years, and he graduated in other disciplines. At Shanyavsky University, Vygotsky presumably studied a broad curriculum of courses in the humanities plus psychology (Vygodskaya and Lifanova 1996). He graduated with a master's thesis on Shakespeare's *Hamlet*, the play that had fascinated him from his adolescent years. The topic of his master's thesis at Moscow University remains unknown but Vygotsky's daughter claims he graduated at both universities, which suggests that Vygotsky finished his law studies as well (Vygodskaya and Lifanova 1996).

Be that as it may, any plans that Vygotsky may have had for his future profession as a lawyer changed radically in the year he finished his studies. It was the *annus terribilis* of 1917, the year that shook Russia and the world, and that still casts its shadows over large parts of Eastern Europe.

Social Turmoil and Cultural Revolution

The October Revolution and the events that followed caused a social havoc that was unprecedented in recent Russian history. Years of both civil and international war plus brutal political repression and 'social reforms' caused a devastation that it will still take Russia many years to recover from. Although we cannot discuss these events in any detail, it would be meaningless to discuss Vygotsky's life and his theories without this background. One result of the upheavals was, for instance, that millions of children lost their parents and homes (the so-called *bezprizorniki*) and roamed the streets causing social inconvenience in the form of begging, theft and prostitution (Stevens 1982). Vygotsky would be one of those involved in finding a solution to this major social problem. Another problem was that as a result of the October Revolution and the civil war about two million Russians fled their country while others were expelled, arrested or killed. Naturally, this created vacancies in all layers of the society that could not always be filled by competent candidates. The result was often chaos and improvisation. Again, Vygotsky participated in the solution of this social problem by giving many courses at various schools and institutions.

But all social revolutions, even the most appalling ones, bring some benefits for most people or many benefits for some. And sometimes it may be difficult to draw the balance. This holds for the October Revolution and its role in Vygotsky's life as well. In Tsarist Russia, he might have become an excellent lawyer or a beloved general practitioner but no academic career would have been possible. In Soviet Russia, academic positions were open to Jews but academic life itself became highly precarious due to the totalitarian aspirations of the communist regime. That raises the question of what Vygotsky himself thought of the October Revolution. In my view, he welcomed several of the social reforms that the new communist regime carried through.

Being a Jew, Vygotsky must have been delighted that the regulations against the Jews were abolished and that now the future was open to him. In addition, it seems clear that he believed that the new system of free education would lead to the emancipation of the hitherto oppressed farmers, workers, and ethnic minorities.[4] After the Revolution, Vygotsky – like many other intellectuals – became immensely active as a teacher of evening courses to uneducated adults. He also seems to have accepted the Marxist worldview (more than its 'application' in Russia, perhaps). In his writings, we find the standard phrases of Marx, Engels and Lenin that were required from intellectuals at the time, but there is also an attempt at genuine theorizing from Marxist premises. Through his work, Vygotsky was also well acquainted with high-ranking Party officials such as the minister of education, Anatoly Lunacharsky, and Lenin's wife, Nadezhda Krupskaya. Meanwhile, (Party) politics in the more narrow sense of the word was not what interested Vygotsky most, or so it seems. A close friend of Vygotsky has even claimed that after the October Revolution Vygotsky wrote several brochures in each of which he objectively set forth the basic views of different political parties (Valsiner and Van der Veer 2000). This suggests a detached view that is difficult to reconcile with the passionate support for one or the other party. In fine, it seems safe to presume that Vygotsky at least initially combined an active interest in Marxist theory with a belief in the new Soviet society. Whether and to what extent he became disillusioned by the events to come remains unknown.

The chain of events that coincided with or were the result of the 1917 revolt had tremendous repercussions on Vygotsky's private life and his career. Apart from the October Revolution itself, he experienced in one way or another World War I, the German and Ukrainian occupation, the civil war, famine, and political repression (Valsiner and Van der Veer 2000). Immediately after his graduation, he returned to Gomel – where his parents and several of his siblings still lived – and tried to earn a living by giving private lessons. It was while taking care of his younger brother in Gomel, who would soon die, that Vygotsky contracted tuberculosis, the disease that haunted him throughout his life and that eventually killed him. Meanwhile, Gomel was being occupied and looted by different armies and warlords. It was only in 1919, after the final liberation of Gomel by the Red Army, that a return to normal life became possible again.

The social upheavals went hand in glove with an upsurge of cultural creativity that was by all standards truly remarkable. In Moscow and St Petersburg, but also in the émigré circles in Berlin, Paris and Prague (Raeff 1990), Russian artists, musicians, poets and novelists created works of art that we still regard as outstanding achievements at a worldclass level. The number and quality of the Russian novelists in the early twentieth century – despite attempts by the authorities to impose what was called 'social realism' – was quite astonishing. Among Vygotsky's contemporaries we find such gifted writers as Babel, Belyj, Bulgakov, Bunin (Nobel Prize 1933), Nabokov, Paustovsky, Platonov, Remizov, Sholokhov and Zamyatin. Remarkable poets such as Akhmatova, Blok, Ehrenburg, Esenin, Khodasevich, Mayakovsky, Mandel'shtam, Pasternak (Nobel Prize 1958), and Tsvetaeva added unforgettable poems to the already rich Russian heritage. Musicians such as Prokofiev, Shostakovich and Stravinsky composed extraordinary new music. The artists Chagall, El-Lissitzky, Kandinsky and Malevich caused a worldwide sensation with their new style of painting. The film director Eisenstein originated a fundamentally new style of filming with his *Battleship Potemkin* (1926). The stage directors Meyerhold, Stanislavsky and Tairov staged unique performances of classic plays. There were new developments in architecture, sculpture and ballet. And so on and so forth. In sum, the Russian avant-garde movement produced a truly bewildering avalanche of works of art that both stunned and shocked the contemporary consumer.

Among the most avid consumers of this dazzling display of artistry was the young student Lev Vygotsky. As we saw above, already in his childhood and youth he kept abreast of the most recent developments in literature, drama, the fine arts, and music. Now, being a student, he missed no opportunity to visit the performances in Tairov's *Chamber Theater* and Meyerhold's and Stanislavsky's *Art Theater*. That active interest in cultural life would remain throughout Vygotsky's life and partly determined the choice of his friends and the nature of his jobs and activities. For example, in 1918, during a stay in Kiev, Vygotsky became acquainted with the poet Ilya Ehrenburg. After he returned from Gomel to Moscow, Vygotsky became a regular visitor of the

Mandelstams and he quoted Osip Mandelstam's poems in his scientific writings even after the latter's arrest by the authorities. During that same period, Vygotsky also befriended the film director Eisenstein and together with Luria they planned several projects. It is likely that Vygotsky met many of the representatives of the cultural elite of that time through the job he acquired at Gomel after he finished his university studies.

The Gomel Period: From Art to Psychology

Above I showed how Vygotsky earned an insecure living by teaching at various schools and giving private lessons after his return to Gomel in 1917. However, around 1920 he managed to get a job as cultural official in Gomel, a position that made his life much easier. In that capacity, he traveled all over Russia to bring the best theatrical companies, poets and novelists to Gomel. He also wrote weekly reviews of theater performances for the local newspapers, co-founded a literary journal and a publishing house, both rather short-lived, and worked for the local Press Museum, which aimed to promote the reading of both the belles-lettres and newspapers (Valsiner and Van der Veer 2000). In sum, Vygotsky displayed enormous activity in a great number of functions and jobs. They were all somehow connected to the goal of raising the cultural level of the public by making available high quality education and the best of Russian and international culture.[5] When we look at the topics that Vygotsky addressed in his numerous lectures and classes, we meet popular subjects (e.g. relativity theory), Russian literature, but also psychology and philosophy, the disciplines he got to know thoroughly at Shanyavsky University.

It was in 1923 that Vygotsky's gradual turn from art to psychology became more visible when he managed to install a small laboratory at the local normal school. He had been teaching at that school, the Gomel Teacher College, for some time and his lectures would later be published as *Educational Psychology* (Vygotsky 1926; see Chapter 2). But now the laboratory allowed him to carry out little experiments with the help of his students, to replicate earlier psychological findings, and to devise investigations of his own. It was the presentation of some of his own findings and his authoritative critique of well-known psychologists during the Second Psychoneurology Congress in Leningrad in 1924 that earned him an invitation to come and work at the Institute of Experimental Psychology at Moscow University (Van der Veer and Valsiner 1991). In themselves, Vygotsky's early investigations were not truly remarkable, but shortly before they were carried out the Institute of Experimental Psychology had been purged, and its new leader, Konstantin Kornilov, urgently needed capable young persons to fill the many vacancies (Van der Veer 2007).

Academic Career

Of course, these new young scientists had to be Marxists as well, because Kornilov's appointment was the result of his campaign against his former teacher Grigoriy Chelpanov, whose ideas had been labeled as 'anti-Marxist' and 'idealist'. However, the labels 'anti-Marxist' and 'Marxist' were very flexible and nobody had any idea what a Marxist psychology should entail. The only thing that was clear in the early 1920s was that 'the authorities' (e.g. one's superior at the university, a friendly colleague active in the Party) demanded a Marxist psychology and that ignoring that demand was not going to advance and might even positively harm one's academic career. The result was predictable: some psychologists just continued their old work under a new heading (among them was Kornilov); others did no more than criticize what now came to be called 'bourgeois', 'anti-Marxist' or 'capitalistic' psychology without offering any new perspectives of their own; still others spiced their more or less productive work with apt quotations from Marx, Engels and Lenin; and, finally, relatively few psychologists sincerely tried to think through what a Marxist psychology might be (Kornilov 1928).

The situation was aggravated by the fact that the authorities regularly launched campaigns against what they saw as ideologically harmful doctrines in the area of philosophy and psychology. Thus, when speaking about the 'soul' had become labeled as an 'idealistic distortion' (e.g. those who used that word supposedly did not understand or accept that the soul must have a material substrate) and psychologists massively hastened to declare that all mental processes are ultimately brain-based, these same psychologists were then suddenly accused of defending 'vulgar materialism', 'abstract reductionism' and so on. Such sudden and unexpected campaigns and the shifts in ideology they entailed caused much confusion, insecurity and ultimately demoralization among researchers, which may have been the intention of the authorities in the first place.[6] Although the debates in Soviet science to some extent resembled genuine scientific discussions, it is best to see them for what they really were: the result of desperate and/or opportunistic attempts by researchers and social activists to save their social position and job or gain a better one by jumping on the right bandwagon at the right time. It took great courage and moral resolve to withstand all this social pressure and to stick to the position that one believed was the scientifically right one and it will come as no surprise that very few people were capable of that. But among these persons, as we will see below, was Vygotsky.

Vygotsky's appointment at the Institute of Experimental Psychology was only the first of a long series of appointments at different institutes in Moscow, Leningrad and Kiev. In fact, one can see that in his academic life he quickly resumed the pattern of frantic educational and social activity that we have seen at Gomel. In the ten years that separated Vygotsky from his death, he would always simultaneously work for publishing houses, edit scientific journals, teach courses at various universities and institutes, act as a clinical psychologist at various clinics, supervise dissertations, work for governmental committees, organize and attend conferences, devise research plans, and write numerous popular and scientific articles and books. The number of activities and the quality of his work is truly remarkable if we realize that all this was accomplished by a person suffering from tuberculosis who at times suffered attacks that incapacitated him for months in a row. In 1926, for example, Vygotsky became ill to the point that he could no longer walk independently, was told that he had no more than a few months to live,[7] and yet during his hospital stay he managed to write large parts of his analysis of the crisis in psychology.

Because Vygotsky is regarded by many as a child psychologist or educational psychologist it may come as a surprise that a large number of his jobs and functions throughout his Moscow period were connected with a different field, namely that of clinical psychology and rehabilitation. Right from the beginning of his stay in Moscow, Vygotsky became involved in the study and treatment of physically disabled and mentally impaired children, a discipline that was called 'defectology' in the Soviet Union. Contemporaries have claimed that he was a remarkable diagnostician who with great tact and gentleness lay bare the problems of disabled or disturbed children. But fairly soon, Vygotsky also developed a new vision of the treatment and rehabilitation of such children and eventually he became accepted as one of the theoretical leaders of Russian defectology.

It would be tedious to list all the positions that Vygotsky held from 1924 to 1934 but I shall mention a number of them, just to give an idea of what this small sickly man could accomplish.

Vygotsky lectured (first as an assistant, and from 1931 as a full professor) at the first and second Moscow State Universities, the Moscow Conservatoire, the Krupskaya Academy for Communist Education, the Moscow Institute for Pedology and Defectology, the Kharkov Psychoneurological Institute, and the Herzen Pedagogical Institute in Leningrad.

Vygotsky's clinical work took place in various institutes where he (for longer or shorter periods) occupied increasingly important administrative positions. He was, for example, head of the Laboratory for the Psychology of Abnormal Childhood of the Medico-Pedagogical Clinic, head of the Experimental Defectological Institute, head of the Laboratory of Sepp's Clinic for Nervous Diseases at the first Moscow State University, and vice-director of the Institute for the Health Care of Children and Adolescents. Shortly before his death, he was offered the position of head of the Psychological Department of the All-Union Institute for Experimental Medicine.

Some of his experimental work Vygotsky carried out at still other scientific institutes, such as the Institute for Experimental Psychology, the Experimental Defectological Institute and the Laboratory for the Experimental Knowledge of Art. And in 1931, he enrolled as a medical student at Kharkov University. He and Luria had decided that to deepen their insight in various clinical problems they had to know more of medicine. So, while a professor of psychology, Vygotsky became a medical student once again (Vygodskaya and Lifanova 1996).

If we combine these activities with his work for journals and publishers, with the work in scientific organizations and committees, with the work with various groups of students and colleagues, with the regular travel by train from Moscow to Leningrad and Kharkov, with the rather poor housing conditions (Vygotsky, his wife and his two children had an apartment of only two rooms and Vygotsky wrote many of his works at home during the night; cf. Vygodskaya and Lifanova 1996), and with his frail health, then we can see that Vygotsky's production of over 200 articles and books is truly impressive. Ignoring the advice of his doctors, he kept working extremely hard and eventually suffered a final attack of tuberculosis that resulted in his demise at the age of 37 on 11 June 1934.[8]

Vygotsky the Man

The biographical notes given above give an impression of Vygotsky's life course but they reveal little of Vygotsky's personality. What kind of man was he? What impression did he leave on his contemporaries? Here again, our information is limited. The little we know or surmise is based on several dozen letters by Vygotsky that survived in various personal archives and on reminiscences by his daughter, colleagues and students. Fortunately for the historian, the people who knew Vygotsky well are almost unanimous in their judgments. Vygotsky seems to have been a very modest, generous and delicate man who treated his patients, students and colleagues with the utmost courtesy and friendliness. He got on exceptionally well with children, both the physically disabled or mentally ill children whom he saw as a clinician, and those free of physical or mental illness. His ability to concentrate and his capacity for work were by all accounts extraordinary: he would discuss scientific topics with students and colleagues in overcrowded rooms, make notes in countless tiny notebooks while traveling on trains and buses, and could explain many issues impromptu in short lectures that were almost ready for print. In fact, many of his scientific papers are based on lectures and sometimes their oral nature is still evident.[9] Vygotsky's classes attracted many students who clearly found his personality and way of speaking most charming even when he sometimes continued much longer than was usual. It was evident to all that this small sickly man lived for his science, that he breathed psychology, and that his one and only goal was to create a new psychology. His feverish activity, his devotion to his work, his contempt for sloppy work and less than full dedication, can only be understood against the following background: here was a man who knew his time was running out fast (after all, tuberculosis was still incurable and doctors had repeatedly announced his approaching death), and who was determined to ignore that banal medical fact and to leave a lasting impression on his science. Against that background we can also understand the elatedness and seriousness of some of his letters to colleagues when he speaks of their common cause, the difficult road they have chosen and the necessity of devoting one's life to the reform of psychology (Luria 1994; Van der Veer and Valsiner 1991). Against that background we can also understand why he was bitterly disappointed when people from his inner circle for political or other reasons decided to take another road, to embrace another theory or philosophy. It is true that to some extent he was armed against such disappointments by his stoic or rationalist[10] approach to life: in his letters to students and colleagues and in personal conversations he claimed that one should always attempt to control one's emotions and subject them to the control of reason. But there are accounts that towards the end of his life, when the political pressure was mounting (e.g. Party committees went through Vygotsky's work in search of suspect views and defamatory articles appeared in the scientific press) and his health was deteriorating, Vygotsky no longer saw a way out of the difficulties and became depressed (Van der Veer and Valsiner 1991; Van der Veer 2000).

The fact that Vygotsky left a group of devoted followers, who after his death, and despite enormous political pressure and, therefore, personal danger, remained faithful to his memory and ideas, must be of some significance as well. It must mean that through his personal charm, moral integrity and intellectual power he made an overwhelming impression on his contemporaries. Apparently, Vygotsky had the gift to gather small groups of students and colleagues who would come to look upon him as their scientific and indeed spiritual leader, and who subsequently would do everything to investigate and promote his ideas. Many of these students and colleagues in retrospect regarded their acquaintance with Vygotsky as a turning point in their life and divided their lives, so to speak, into a pre-Vygotskian and post-Vygotskian part (cf. Luria 1979; 1982). Taken together, these facts suggest that this man, with his strangely shaven head,[11] was both spiritually and intellectually a remarkable individual towards whom few could remain indifferent.

Political Pressure

I have repeatedly mentioned that being a psychologist in the Soviet Union of the 1920s and 1930s was a difficult and sometimes dangerous thing. To be and remain a professional psychologist in that period required considerable skills, flexibility and luck. Psychologists, and people in general, were arrested on completely arbitrary grounds, not just because they did not toe the Party line. With hindsight, one can see that there was plenty of material that might have led to Vygotsky's arrest.

First, he had the wrong social (middle-class) and ethnic background. Persons with a 'bourgeois' background, especially those proficient in foreign languages, were arrested in great numbers in the late 1930s, and Jews again became the victim of prosecution in the 1940s (cf. McLeish 1975).

Second, Vygotsky had written positively about or been friendly with individuals who subsequently became branded as 'enemies of the people'. These included politicians, (foreign) researchers and poets. Most prominent among these persons was Leon Trotsky, whom Vygotsky repeatedly and approvingly quoted in his major works. Trotsky, as is well known, became Stalin's arch-enemy, was forced to leave the country, and was eventually murdered by a Soviet agent in Mexico City in August 1940. Among the researchers, whom Vygotsky knew personally or positively referred to, we find the literary critic Yuli

Aikhenvald and the philosopher Semyon Frank, who were both expelled for their political views in 1922 (Chamberlain 2006). Other politically suspect figures whom Vygotsky knew personally were the poet Osip Mandel'shtam, arrested in May 1934, and his cousin David Vygodsky, arrested in February 1938. Both died in concentration camps.

Third, Vygotsky had shown a preference for scientific currents that subsequently became unmasked as utterly unscientific. These included psychoanalysis and pedology. By the late 1930s, psychoanalysis and pedology, but also reactology, reflexology, industrial psychology, social psychology and forensic psychology, had fallen into disgrace (Strakhov 1930; Talankin 1931; Vedenov 1932).

However, the fact is that Vygotsky was not arrested. What saved him? We still do not know enough to answer that question. From Vygotsky's private correspondence, we know that a public meeting on the topic of his views was in the making. We know that a research project carried out in Uzbekistan caused Vygotsky and Luria many difficulties (see Chapter 5) and we know that articles critical of Vygotsky's view began appearing in the scientific press from about 1931. It is these articles that give us the best impression of the mounting political pressure.

What did these critics say about Vygotsky's ideas? I will give but a few examples (cf. Van der Veer 2000; Van der Veer and Valsiner 1991). Feofanov (1932) claimed, among other things, that Vygotsky neglected the class environment in his theorizing about children's mental development and found his theory 'eclectic' (the catchword in that historical period). Abel'skaya and Neopikhonova (1932) argued that Vygotsky's concept of a 'cultural tool' (see Chapter 3) was non-Marxist because it ignored production relations. Razmyslov (1934), as head of a committee that investigated Vygotsky's work, objected to Vygotsky's and Luria's characterization of the mental processes of Uzbeks. He also observed that early statements by Vygotsky and Luria were not in agreement with recent Party decrees (Van der Veer 2000). Kozyrev and Turko (1936), among other things, argued that Vygotsky's analysis of the different roots of thinking and speech were not in accord with Engels'. They attacked Vygotsky's followers using words such as 'class vigilance', 'fascism', 'enemy' and 'self-criticism'. Finally, Rudneva (1937) noted that Vygotsky had introduced fascist ideas into Soviet psychology. Like the other critics, she attempted to discredit Vygotsky by demonstrating that his ideas were not in accord with the Marxist classics, recent Party decrees, casual remarks by Stalin, and so on.

Taken together, these publications sketch a disheartening and hair-raising picture of the development of ideological control in Soviet psychology in the 1930s. It is clear that ultimately the question whether a theory was acceptable or true had become equivalent to the question whether that theory was in accord with statements made by Marx, Engels, Lenin, Stalin, or the latest decisions of the Central Committee of the Communist Party.

The publications also make clear that Vygotsky's position had become increasingly difficult by the time of his death. The posthumous criticisms, in particular, strongly suggest that he would not have been able to continue his work after 1936. Moreover, had he lived on, he might have been arrested and perished in the Gulag Archipelago. It is probable that his death from tuberculosis in a way saved him from a more horrible death. In that respect his situation in 1934 was reminiscent of that of Kafka ten year earlier. 'Kill me', Kafka said to his doctor when he lay dying of tuberculosis, 'else you are a murderer'. Vygotsky faced similar options and was lucky to die of a natural disease in the company of his relatives. The disease killed him; otherwise he might have been murdered.

Notes

1. As an adolescent, Vygodsky changed his name into Vygotsky, for reasons that remain unknown. All the other members of his family, including his two daughters, have kept the original name.
2. The Pale of Settlement (Russian: *Cherta osedlosti*) was created by Catherine the Great in 1791. The area extended from the *pale* or demarcation line, to the border with Europe and included a part of Poland, White Russia, Lithuania, Ukraine, and Crimea. Even

within this area Jews were discriminated against, for example, having to pay double taxes. The Pale was abolished after the October Revolution.
3. Until a few years ago, Jews were viewed as an ethnic category (a 'nationality' as it was called) and that category was noted in the Russian passport.
4. Vygotsky wrote a very favorable review of John Reed's (1919) rather one-dimensional book on the October Revolution, called *Ten Days that Shook the World* (Vygotsky 1923d).
5. In a sense, Vygotsky continued the social activity of his father who – as we have seen – was instrumental in founding the local library.
6. The point is that it was increasingly expected, indeed demanded, that researchers would actively criticize their colleagues along the Party lines both during public meetings and in the scientific press (e.g., 'In his article comrade Ivanov has grossly distorted Lenin's brilliant insights and objectively [= effectively] defended a vulgar-materialist view') and would be subjected to the same critique by their equally opportunistic colleagues. In the end, few researchers could withstand the tremendous pressure, and double-speak and cynical obedience became the rule (cf. Van der Veer 2000).
7. Apparently, he was subjected to the pneumothorax technique, i.e. the artificial collapsing of an infected lung to rest it and allow lesions to heal, but as usual this had few beneficial effects.
8. No effective treatment for tuberculosis existed at the time and about half of the patients eventually died.
9. Although Vygotsky's writings are very lucid and although he can be viewed as a brilliant thinker, I personally do not regard him as one of the best psychological writers in the literary sense of the word. I suspect Vygotsky hardly ever devoted much time to the stylistic qualities of his writings (rewriting and polishing them endlessly as some do) – perhaps thinking he had no time for that – and thus did not match the level of, say, William James in his *Principles of Psychology* or Pierre Janet in his *Psychological Healing*.
10. Vygotsky's personal variant of stoicism was strongly influenced by his repeated readings of Spinoza's *Ethics*, a book that he received

as a present from his father when he was an adolescent (Van der Veer and Valsiner 1991; Vygodskaya and Lifanova 1996).
11. Vygotsky was in the habit of shaving his head in the summer, which was quite unusual at that time. See the remark by the film director Eisenstein in Luria (1994, p. 39).

Part 2

Critical Exposition of Vygotsky's Work

Chapter 2

Early Writings

Hamlet

In Chapter 1 I have shown that the young Vygotsky became fascinated by literature and theatre and that it was through thinking about the problem of artistic creation that he arrived at psychology. In this chapter I shall discuss this transition from art to psychology in some detail and pay attention to the subject matter of his thinking and writing in the period that runs from 1915 to 1924, the year that Vygotsky moved to Moscow. Unfortunately, not all of Vygotsky's writings from this period are known to us. Throughout his student years, and even more so while working in Gomel, Vygotsky published reviews of books he read, plays he attended and so on. About 90 of these brief notices in different journals and newspapers have so far been discovered, mostly from Vygotsky's Gomel period, but very few of them have been republished in any language. Personally, I have read but a dozen of them. That means that for our reconstruction we must primarily rely on the two major writings that have been republished, notably Vygotsky's master's thesis on *Hamlet* and his dissertation on the psychology of art, neither of which were published during Vygotsky's lifetime.

Of Vygotsky's master's thesis there exist two versions, both handwritten manuscripts in notebooks. The first draft was written in Gomel in August–September 1915 and the second and final version in Moscow in February–March 1916. The title of the thesis was *The Tragedy of Hamlet, Prince of Denmark, by W. Shakespeare* and in printed form its length is about 175 pages. For a young man of only 19 years old it is a remarkably mature work. The text is well written, the argumentation is consistent and even for readers who do not agree with his viewpoints it is clear that the author speaks with authority. From the dozens of footnotes it becomes apparent that Vygotsky had read a vast amount of the existing literature about *Hamlet* and Shakespeare and was acquainted with many of the interpretations of the play. Furthermore, an immediate source of inspiration were the performances of *Hamlet* staged by Konstantin Stanislavsky (1853–1938)[1] and Edward Gordon Craig (1872–1966) in the Moscow Art Theatre (MKhAT) from December 1911 to March 1914 (Senelick 1982; Yaroshevsky 1989; 1993). However, in his lengthy analysis of *Hamlet* Vygotsky did not refer to the massive secondary literature he read in the main text of his work, but only in the footnotes. This was connected with the very special approach to literary critique that he adopted in his thesis.

The view defended by Vygotsky was that a critique of *Hamlet* may be entirely subjective and need not discuss other, different critiques. Each reader is in a way an author himself, because each reader creates his own *Hamlet*. Shakespeare's play is just a potential to be realized by each reader anew and sometimes the readers' impressions are deeper and more true than what the author could say about his text. Different readings of the play can co-exist peacefully and there is no need to attack other interpretations. Still, according to Vygotsky – who was following the ideas of the Russian literary critics Alexander Gornfeld (cf. 1916; 1923) and Yuly Aikhenvald (cf. 1910; 1922)[2] – there are some rules to obey when interpreting a literary text such as a play: (1) the interpretation must be based on just the play under scrutiny; (2) it must be original; (3) it must be consistent; and (4) it must not provide a rational explanation of the piece but just express impressions. The point is that Vygotsky (and the persons he was inspired by) wanted to retain what he called the mystery of the play; the truth that they claimed cannot be expressed in words. In that view, plays – or works of art in general – cannot be reduced to motives, to what the artist supposedly really wanted to say. In his preface, Vygotsky remarked that his thesis was actually the middle part of a trilogy yet to be written. The first part would deal with all the scholarly critique of *Hamlet*, research about the authorship of Shakespeare's plays, and so on. The third and final part would give a religious interpretation of the play. To the best of our knowledge, these other parts have never been written.

Vygotsky's analysis of *Hamlet* itself was essentially a scene-by-scene interpretation of the play in which he consistently emphasized the unreal, ghostly, other-worldly nature of the events that take place.

Vygotsky began his discussion with a description of the strange light that can be seen when the night is over but the day has not yet begun. A light that makes everything seem diffuse, mysterious and somehow sad. This light is characteristic of the play and its mysterious and sad nature. In Vygotsky's account, Hamlet is in between day and night, a citizen of two worlds, so to speak, namely the terrestrial world of the here and the now and the world of the afterlife which hides a terrible secret that cannot be grasped by living people. Hamlet somehow senses something of the terrible secret of the other world and his behavior is dictated by it. It is as if he were in a trance, as if he were behaving automatically. The other persons in the play also seem to act unknowingly and unwillingly, as if they were puppets on a string. Whether active (the king) or passive (the others), the characters act as blind men who cannot prevent the denouement of the tragedy. Fundamentally and forever lonely, they do not understand each other. And behind the apparent actions of these lonely people there is some mysterious clockwork. Or, in Vygotsky's words:

> In each tragedy, behind the violent whirlpool of human passions, debility, love and hate, behind the scenes of passionate strivings and misunderstandings we hear the remote echoes of a mystic symphony speaking about what is ancient, intimate and beloved.
> (Vygotsky 1986, p. 487)

Vygotsky concluded that he had not unriddled *Hamlet* but that that had never been his intention. The purpose of his thesis was just to draw the reader's attention to one possible and admittedly subjective interpretation of the play while preserving its mysterious character.

Vygotsky's interpretation followed the rules he himself had stipulated. That is, it was original, consistent, impressionistic, and made no claims that were based on the reading of other works by Shakespeare. But although it was a unique analysis, it nevertheless was very characteristic of that timeframe. As Yaroshevsky (1987) and others have pointed out, mystic and religious thinkers and novelists were quite popular in the early twentieth century in Russia. The ideas that life is absurd, that persons do not really know each other, that everybody is ultimately lonely, that there must be 'something more', and so on, were quite common. Many intellectuals visited spiritualistic séances where dancing tables communicated messages from the non-dimensional world to talented mediums. Others (e.g. V.V. Rozanov, N.A. Berdyaev) developed religious-philosophical views of their own making. There was much popular interest in the bizarre phenomena that can be called forth by hypnosis (cf. Valsiner and Van der Veer 2000). Obscure thinkers, such as Rudolf Steiner (anthroposophy) and Samuel Hahnemann (homeopathy), enjoyed certain popularity. In fine, it was a period during which intellectuals openly expressed their interest in spiritual and occult affairs. Against that background, Vygotsky's youthful interpretation of Hamlet was not remarkable but – although unique in its details – typical of the *Zeitgeist*. Of course, over the next decades the expression of all philosophical and religious views other than Marxism would become increasingly difficult and the memory of dancing tables would fade in time.

Psychology of Art

We now take a major step from Vygotsky's master's thesis written in 1916 to his doctoral dissertation submitted in 1925. As related in Chapter 1, this period was largely spent in Gomel where Vygotsky worked as an organizer of cultural events, a literary critic, a teacher, and so on. Having returned to Moscow in 1924, Vygotsky now devoted his time primarily to psychology. His talks, articles and chapters from the period 1924–5 focused almost exclusively on matters of general and clinical psychology. However, when Vygotsky in 1925 suffered another severe attack of tuberculosis and was confined to bed for months in a row, he used this opportunity to write a PhD making use of the knowledge and insights he had gathered in the preceding ten years. The result was *The Psychology of Art* (1925), which was not defended in public in view of his state of health and never published during Vygotsky's lifetime, despite a signed contract with a publisher (Van der Veer and Valsiner 1991). It is while reading *The Psychology of Art* that we can clearly see that Vygotsky's thinking had undergone major changes in the years that had elapsed after the October Revolution (cf. Ivanov 1986).

Right from the start of his doctoral dissertation Vygotsky asserts that we should avoid the subjectivism so characteristic of his own earlier approach to the psychology of art. Rather than emphasizing that works of art are ultimately enigmatic and that aesthetic appreciation is in the eye of the beholder, he now claimed that artistic creations are systems of stimuli carefully organized to evoke certain aesthetic reactions. Thus, in order to understand the aesthetic effects caused by a piece of art we must first of all understand the artist's technique, the subtle interplay between form and content that creates emotional conflicts and tension and ultimately catharsis in the recipient. Before elaborating this view, Vygotsky first dealt with several theories that he found inadequate. He rejected the view – which he attributed to Alexander Potebnya (1989), his former teacher Gustav Shpet (1989), and ultimately to Wilhelm von Humboldt – that it is the content or material that is of primary importance in art. Likewise, he criticized the view advanced by the founders of the Russian formalist schools, Viktor Shklovsky, Boris Eikhenbaum, Roman Yakobson, Yury Tynyanov, and others, that it is primarily style or form that determines the aesthetic reaction. Agreeing with Shklovsky that art is a technique or device (Russian: *priem*), a specific form of poetic language, Vygotsky nevertheless argued that there is more to art than just form. In his opinion, it was exactly the artificially created conflict between form and content that created the artistic effect (Vygotsky 1986; 1987).

To argue that view, Vygotsky analyzed three forms of art, notably the fable, the short story and the tragedy. According to Vygotsky, each of these genres confirmed his view. Characteristic of fables – Vygotsky analyzed the fables of Ivan Krylov – is that they evoke contradictory emotions that are finally resolved in the denouement or punchline, which Vygotsky compared to a short circuit. For example, in one of Krylov's fables a lamb defends itself against a wolf's accusations. The more successful the lamb becomes in its plea the more one feels its imminent death approaching. And in the end the tension between the feeling of increasing hope (caused by the lamb's successful arguments) and the feeling of growing danger is resolved by the wolf's words 'You are guilty, because I am hungry.'

Something similar happens in the short story, according to Vygotsky. To prove his point, he analyzed the short story *Gentle Breath* by the Russian poet and novelist Ivan Bunin who would win the Nobel Prize for literature in 1933. It is the story of a high-school girl who is seduced by an elderly acquaintance and some time later is shot by another lover when she refuses to marry him and ridicules him. In between these dramatic events the girl tells a classmate that she read in an old book that attractive girls (apart from other physical properties) should have a gentle breath, which she claims to have. Characteristic of the story is that the material (or content, or plot) of the story – i.e. a girl is seduced, tells a classmate that she has a gentle breath, begins another affair, ridicules her lover, is shot by that lover – is not told in that order. That is, the material is rearranged by the writer in a certain form. Vygotsky argued that this rearrangement by Bunin was crucial in achieving certain aesthetic effects in the reader. By destroying the chronological order of events Bunin avoided a growing tension in the reader and achieved a certain lightness or gentleness of style[3] that stands in sharp contrast with the sad content of the story. According to Vygotsky, Bunin's final line 'And now this gentle breath is dissipated again in the world, in the cloud-covered sky, in this cold spring wind' resolves the contradiction between form and content of the story.

For his analysis of the third art form, the tragedy, Vygotsky returned to his beloved *Hamlet*. This time, however, there is no mention of its other-worldliness, of its religious character, and neither does Vygotsky claim that each reader creates his own *Hamlet*. And the enigmatic character of Shakespeare's play he now regarded as the result of an intentional artistic device that we must try to understand. Again, it was achieved by the poet's subtle play with form and content, according to Vygotsky. On the one hand, we have the simple story of Hamlet, who must avenge his father by killing the king. This is a straightforward chain of events that everybody expects to happen. However, Shakespeare diverts from this preset path with many digressions that delay the unfolding of the simple plot. The line of action constantly meanders in quite complex curves, strays from the path set by that plot and thereby creates tensions in the recipient who is all the time experiencing the contradictions between the logical and the actual course of events. Moreover, in a tragedy more than in the fable or short story, the reader identifies with the hero and watches the events taking place both through the hero's eyes and through his own, which again creates a conflict. This led Vygotsky to the following remark:

> In the fable we discovered two meanings within one and the same action. In the short story we discovered one level for the story (subject) and one for the plot (material). In the tragedy we uncover yet another level, the psyche and the emotions of the hero. Since all three levels refer in the last analysis to the same facts taken in three different contexts, it is obvious that they must contradict one another.
> (Vygotsky 1925/1971, pp. 192–3)

And Vygotsky concluded that again, just like in the fable and the short story, the aesthetic effects produced by a tragedy such as *Hamlet* are the result of artful device: the readers are led to contradictory expectations, which creates a tension that is only resolved in the final lines. This leads to a discharge of nervous energy that may be called catharsis.

In the remaining chapters of his dissertation Vygotsky tried to corroborate his hypothesis by concisely dealing with other stories and plays and philosophized about the meaning of art in social life. These chapters did not yield any new full-fledged theories but they were nevertheless interesting in that they mentioned some themes that were to be of fundamental importance in Vygotsky's later work. Thus, Vygotsky claimed that art is a social tool or technique that brings the most intimate and personal aspects of our being into the sphere of social life. 'The social', Vygotsky (1925/1971, p. 249) remarked, 'also exists where there is only one person with his individual experiences and tribulations'. He also prophesized that 'new art' will play a role in creating the new Soviet man. Both the notion of social or cultural tool and the notion of the fundamental social nature of our most private thoughts and emotions he would develop further in the years to come. And exclamations about the role of psychology (or art, or education) in the betterment of man were to embellish the final passages of his books for some years to come.

When we compare Vygotsky's youthful analysis of *Hamlet* with his dissertation on art we see a great deal of changes. Gone is the emphasis on the enigmatic character of art, the allusions to the hereafter, the subjective creation of art by the recipient, and so on. In its place come references to hard-boiled thinkers (e.g. Bekhterev, Darwin, Pavlov, Sherrington), speculations about the role of art in the creation of the new man (inspired by Plekhanov and Trotsky) and, above all, the analysis of the formal properties of the work of art and its uses to establish certain emotions in the reader and spectator. There is no doubt then that Vygotsky had gone with the tide of events: by 1925 the prevailing view was that psychology should be objective and materialistic. The once popular flirtations with spirits and ghosts had been swept away by talk about reflexes and brains. Those who still did believe in religious values, spiritual qualities and so on had been imprisoned, sent away or silenced. Now it was the time of constructing the new Soviet state, the time of belief in social progress by social and technical engineering, the time of undoing social inequality and injustice, the time to create a new man or even superman. And to that immense choir of enthusiastic socialist believers singing the song of people's progress Vygotsky had joined his own unique voice.

Educational Psychology

Teachers and schools cannot and have never been able to undo social inequality and injustice but they can play a role in creating the worldview and personality of the child. Hence the interest of both democratic and totalitarian states in controlling public education and the need for reforms of the educational system after major societal changes. The Soviet Union formed no exception to this rule: now the Tsarist schools were seen as positively harmful and obsolete in that they spread bourgeois values and religious ideas. Teachers were fired at all levels of the educational system and new curricula were developed. Naturally, a key role in the transition to a new system of education was played by the normal schools or teacher training colleges. After all, it was there that the new teachers were being trained. One of these colleges was located in Gomel and one of the teachers at that Gomel Teacher Training College was Lev Vygotsky. It was at that college that Vygotsky performed his first psychological investigations in a laboratory that he had installed and it was there that he wrote a psychological textbook for his students. This textbook, *Educational Psychology: A Brief Course*, was published in 1926, that is, several years after Vygotsky had moved to Moscow University. Incidentally, it was one of the very few books penned by Vygotsky that would be published during his lifetime.

Educational Psychology (Vygotsky 1926) testifies of the enormous changes that Russian psychology had undergone after the October Revolution. In itself it followed a format that is now quite standard for introductory psychology textbooks in that it dealt with the usual topics of memory, perception, thinking, emotion, and so on. But new for that time was the mixture of a strong emphasis on the material basis of all human behavior and social progressivist ideas phrased in militant prose. Time and again Vygotsky emphasized that human beings are made of the material stuff of nervous tissue, endocrine glands, muscles, etc. This material stuff functions in ways that are determined by heredity, but the social environment is enormously powerful in molding that functioning according to pre-established goals. In particular, Vygotsky believed that it was possible to combine the viewpoints of Darwin, Pavlov and Marx.

In what way did Vygotsky merge the ideas of these major thinkers into a coherent picture of the human being? First, Vygotsky argued with Darwin that human beings are the product of a long evolution and that they have a good deal in common with other primates. Second, Vygotsky argued with Pavlov that human beings are born with a set of innate reflexes that can be coupled with environmental stimuli to produce so-called conditional reflexes.[4] That is, just as a dog can be taught to salivate on hearing a bell or even on hearing specific words (rather than on seeing or tasting delicious food), human beings can be taught to smile when they see their mother or hear her name. The original stimulus that elicits the response can be replaced by an arbitrary new stimulus provided the original stimulus and the new one have been presented to the animal a sufficient number of times. This process of 'classical conditioning' made famous by the teachings of Ivan Pavlov was fully accepted by Vygotsky. In fact, in this period of his career he claimed its supreme importance. In his view, Pavlov had shown that in a carefully arranged environment animals (and therefore humans as well) can be taught all sorts of new things by linking their innate reflexes with new environmental stimuli. In this way, Vygotsky said, Pavlov bridged the existing gulf between biology and sociology. Its importance for education was that the school and the world at large are in fact comparable to Pavlov's laboratory: the teacher can arrange an environment that fundamentally changes the child's original repertoire of reactions. But what kind of environment? That brings us to the third major thinker used by Vygotsky, Karl Marx. His work comes in in the traditional way, when Vygotsky discusses the class character of the Tsarist educational system, its bourgeois moral values and so on, but also in a more subtle way when Vygotsky discusses the fundamental difference between the human and the animal mind. For animals, matters are simple: the behavioral repertoire of the animal must consist of innate behaviors plus the new behaviors learned by that individual animal in the course of its life. These new behaviors Vygotsky considered conditional reflexes. Hence we can express the animal's mind in a simple equation: mind is innate reflexes plus conditional reflexes (which in themselves are the result of the linking of innate reflexes to environmental stimuli).[5] For human beings the situation is incomparably more complex. After all, human beings are not dependent on just their own innate equipment and their individual experience. In addition to innate and conditional reactions they have historical experience, social experience and doubled experience. With the term 'social experience' Vygotsky referred to the fact that human beings are able to profit from the experiences gathered in their collective past. In contradistinction to animals we can learn from history. With the term 'social experience' Vygotsky referred to the fact that we know many facts not from personal experience but relying on the experience of others. The example Vygotsky gives is that of knowing about the Sahara without having been there oneself. Thus, the terms 'historical experience' and 'social experience' seem to refer to the dimensions of time and distance: by historical experience we can overcome time and learn from the past; by social experience we can overcome distance and learn from experiences gathered elsewhere. Finally, there is what Vygotsky coined 'doubled experience' (Russian: *udvoennyj opit*) or consciousness. It is here that Vygotsky referred to Marx, who had claimed that the difference between animals and human beings is that human beings in working carry out a pre-established plan. The finished product first existed as a mental image or intention in the mind and therefore Vygotsky speaks of a 'doubling' of experience. Thus, Vygotsky concluded that the human mind consists of innate reactions plus conditional reflexes plus historical experience plus social experience plus doubled experience.[6] What we can see from these first and rather crude attempts to distinguish animals from human beings is that Vygotsky sought to define humans as biosocial beings. Just like animals we consist of flesh, bones, nervous tissue, glands, and so on but in addition to that we consciously live in a social and physical environment that is shaped by our history and culture. In later years he would come back to the problem of the animal–human difference time and again and eventually he would arrive at what he saw as its definite solution in his cultural-historical theory of the higher functions.

In a book that was meant for future teachers it was inevitable that Vygotsky would deal with the nature of learning and with different educational philosophies. A first thing to note is that he did not want to do away with schools as such. This is of some relevance, because after the October Revolution there were Soviet experts who advocated the discontinuation of all schools as harmful remnants of the Tsarist past and who argued that life is the best teacher. This was definitely not Vygotsky's line of reasoning. His view was that life may teach children many harmful things and that children need schools for moral, aesthetic, intellectual guidance. Schools are there to influence the children's development in favorable ways, to create 'man as a social type' out of 'man as a biological type' (Vygotsky 1930/1997, p. 58). However, it is the child who develops and it is the child who is learning. The teacher's role in that process is necessarily rather modest: (just like Pavlov in his laboratory) he must create an environment that for the children facilitates their learning process. In such an environment, children will in some fundamental sense be actively educating themselves. Just like we cannot stimulate the plant's growth by pulling at its stem or leafs, we cannot force children to learn something, Vygotsky argued. It is the children who are learning by actively processing information imparted or made available by the teacher or obtained on his or her suggestion. In this context, Vygotsky mentioned the idea of the Dalton schools favorably. The application of newly acquired knowledge in the context of work is one way to guarantee its deep-level processing. In this connection, Vygotsky discussed the various types of labor schools and sketched the outlines of what he called a 'polytechnic school'. Such a school would be integrated with productive work in highly developed factories or firms: the children would be introduced to all aspects of the whole production process and the subjects taught would allow them to understand that process and to innovate it by making new discoveries and inventions. The school would embody an ideal of training for science with an eye to immediate practical applications. Vygotsky stated that such schools did not yet exist and agreed with Blonsky (1919/1979) that existing schools were no more than a perversion of the ideal of a polytechnic school.[7]

We thus see that Vygotsky combined a utopian vision of society with a view of education that stressed restraint by the teacher and active participation by the pupil. Pupils fundamentally educate themselves and in the distant future schools may eventually merge with society to create the 'new Soviet man'. I am not sure that Vygotsky's philosophy of education at this time was fully consistent or clear. There seems to be some tension between his general claim that human beings are not dependent on their own experience and his educational claim that we only learn by our own experience. One may, of course, plead – as Vygotsky did – for a modest role of the teacher as being no more than a facilitator or organizer of the pupils' environment. One may stress – as Vygotsky seemed to do – that knowledge is understood and retained best if it is acquired in a process of active acquisition by the child. But it is very important to define what we mean by that active acquisition of knowledge. Vygotsky himself emphasized that one of the distinguishing characteristics between human beings and animals is that human beings inherit social and historical experience. That is, they do not have to discover themselves that the Sahara is a very dry area and that in former times it was not yet a desert. These facts can be explained by the teacher or read in a book. Vygotsky seemed to imply that this is a suboptimal way of acquiring new knowledge. However, it is not clear to me that it is. First, it is dangerous to equate the terms 'active' and 'passive' with certain activities: students may be intellectually very active while listening to a lecture or reading a book. Second, it is not entirely clear what an active acquisition of social and historical knowledge would entail.[8] The least one can say is that Vygotsky did not spell out what his general claims about the role of the teacher in school and the importance of giving free reign to the activity of the child meant for the practice of teaching.

Educational Psychology marked an important stage in Vygotsky's thinking. It reflected a period during which he was much impressed by the discoveries of Pavlov and referred positively to the work of the American behaviorists Karl Lashley and John Watson. Hugo Münsterberg's (1920, pp. 124–5) claim that 'The development of our reactions is our life history . . . If we were to seek an expression for the most important truth which modern psychology can furnish the teacher, it would simply be this: the pupil is a reaction apparatus' even served as the motto of Vygotsky's book. The work of these researchers seemed to provide examples of rigorous experimental work on materialist premises. At the same time Vygotsky raised topics that were anathema to behaviorist die-hards. He claimed that there are fundamental differences between animals and human beings (thus restricting the value of much behaviorist research), he raised the topic of consciousness, and emphasized the role of society in creating the new man. Very soon he would distance himself from the writings of Pavlov, Bekhterev and Watson and point to their very restricted value for the study of human beings. But other themes announced in *Educational Psychology* would continue to play a role in his writings. Time and again, Vygotsky would come back to the issue of animal–human differences; time and again he would stress the importance of human consciousness. But the way he dealt with these issues would substantially change and his work would gradually lose its utopian flavor.

Chapter 3

Creating Cultural-historical Theory

Blind and Deaf Children

It is not generally known that throughout his academic career Vygotsky worked as a clinical psychologist and that his theorizing was inspired by his thinking about the problems experienced by blind, deaf and mentally impaired children. Nevertheless, the diagnosis and treatment of these children formed part of his practical and theoretical activities right from the start of his work at the Institute of Psychology in Moscow. It was in the context of his working with these children that Vygotsky hit upon the notion of the *cultural tool*, one of the key concepts of his later cultural-historical theory.

Take the case of blind children. In order to partake of our culture and to develop intellectually, these children must learn to read. Obviously, they cannot read in the ordinary sense of the word, that is, they cannot translate conventional signs into words and meanings when these are presented visually. However, there is no need to present these signs visually; one may make use of the intact tactile sense of blind children and teach them the Braille script instead. In a sense, then, blind children are just unlucky that our culture happens to prefer the visual presentation of signs to convey information. There is no logical necessity to do it that way as the Braille script proves. What happens is that our cultural way of doing things doesn't suit the particular children. When we look at the child in isolation, we may conclude that the child is physically disabled, but when we look at the child-culture system, we realize that there is a mismatch and that the adoption of another cultural convention removes the mismatch and allows the child to read without any problems. In other words, over the centuries cultures have developed cultural tools or conventions that suit the majority of people (and that may have major advantages) but that cause problems for certain subgroups.

A similar thing can be said about deaf children. These children cannot partake in ordinary conversations, because the conventional way of conducting a conversation is by use of vocal speech. Again, there is no logical necessity to converse by use of vocal speech (although there may be many advantages to that method), because one may use sign language. And again, one might argue that the problem is not so much with the child but with the mismatch between child and cultural convention. As soon as one realizes that, one may teach the child sign language and the child will henceforward have no problems whatsoever conducting conversations providing that the other person understands his or her language. This may seem an extreme point of view (obviously, blind and deaf children have more problems than the mismatches in the domains of reading and speaking), but for Vygotsky the quintessential point was that physically disabled/mentally impaired children experience difficulties with conventional cultural methods or tools and that these may be remedied by devising other cultural tools. In a sense, then, part of the difficulties physically disabled/mentally impaired children experience are the result of a mismatch between their natural abilities and the dominating culture. A similar view was recently defended by Sacks (1989, p. 117), who argued that 'deafness as such is not the affliction; affliction enters with the breakdown of communication and language'.

One of the reasons why Vygotsky dealt with these children and emphasized this particular point was the immense value he attached to children's getting access to our common cultural heritage. Children who cannot communicate with others or cannot read written sources of information will be cut off from fundamentally human means of transmitting information (speech and literacy), which may seriously disadvantage their intellectual development. It is here that Vygotsky made a distinction between blind and deaf children that we now think was erroneous. In the case of blind children, Vygotsky saw no insurmountable problems: the child reading Braille will have access to all major facts, abstract concepts and theories of our culture and hence will not experience any problems in their intellectual development. In the case of deaf children, however, Vygotsky saw an obstacle: we may, as explained above, teach deaf children sign language but this language is inferior to oral language in that it lacks many of the latter's abstract concepts. Teaching a deaf child sign language might thus hamper the child's intellectual development. For this reason Vygotsky advocated teaching deaf children oral speech.[9] Another reason why Vygotsky preferred to teach deaf children oral speech was his fear that the children would become socially isolated if taught signed language. This theme of social isolation and social compensation (through the introduction of other cultural means) was central to Vygotsky's thinking about physically disabled/mentally impaired children at this time. His idea was that these children would not feel inferior or isolated if society took the necessary measures. For this reason he also advocated mainstreaming physically disabled/mentally impaired children if at all possible and was critical of special education (while admitting that for some groups, e.g. deeply mentally impaired children, it was indispensable). Of course, we may see some tension in Vygotsky's thinking about this topic. On the one hand, the experiences with communities of deaf people seem to illustrate that feelings of isolation and inferiority indeed greatly diminish or fully disappear in such groups, which illustrates Vygotsky's assertion that feelings of isolation and inferiority are of social origin and that the living together of physically disabled/mentally impaired children may be beneficial. On the other hand, it is precisely the living together of minorities that tends to consolidate disadvantages and discriminatory labels as Vygotsky also posited. In other words, in Vygotsky's thinking we witness the tension that is still very much present in any decision about mainstream or special education for minority groups.

Primitive and Feeble-minded Children

In his work with children with physical and mental disabilities Vygotsky came across another group that also inspired his theoretical thinking: mentally impaired children. These children were classified as mentally impaired on the basis of different tests. However, on closer inspection it appeared that the group of mentally impaired children actually consisted of two subgroups, those of so-called 'primitive' children and those of congenitally feeble-minded children. This distinction went back to Petrova (1925). Petrova had presented children with syllogisms, asked them to find the generic term for a group of objects, to define concepts, and so on. She found that certain children refused to argue from hypothetical premises, i.e. they refused to draw conclusions from premises that described situations they did not know from their own experience. Also, when asked to classify or define objects, the children tended to concentrate on concrete properties or functional usage rather than discerning abstract properties. For example, if presented with pictures of a cat, a mouse, a horse, and a robin, and asked which three of the four animals belong together, they would invariably say that the cat, the mouse and the robin belong together, because the cat catches both the mouse and the robin. The idea that cat, mouse and horse might be grouped together (because they are mammals rather than birds) was beyond their comprehension.

Petrova argued that such an inability to classify or define objects according to abstract properties did not necessarily reflect a low degree of giftedness or feeble-mindedness. On the basis of an analysis of the children's answers she concluded that some children were highly intelligent but lacked a certain training or education. These children she called *primitive*, borrowing a term used by the ethnologists Lévy-Bruhl (1922/1976) and Thurnwald (1922) to describe non-western types of thinking. The children would overcome their limitations if offered the right type of education. Primitive children should be distinguished from feeble-minded children who as the result of some organic defect are unable to acquire advanced modes of thinking no matter what education they receive.

Vygotsky accepted Petrova's distinction and interpreted it in terms of his notion of a cultural tool. Both groups of children had failed to acquire the necessary cultural tools required for higher abstract thinking but for different reasons. The prognosis of the primitive children was good, because if provided with adequate education they would simply pick up the necessary cultural tools and perform as ordinary children. The prognosis of feeble-minded children was much worse, because these children due to their inherent inabilities had great difficulties acquiring advanced modes of thinking. Again, Vygotsky was inclined to regard this situation as the result of a mismatch. The existing cultural tools of thinking are within reach of the majority of people but may result in problems for a minority. The defects of feeble-minded children would be far less visible in a society that does not put such heavy demands on literacy and abstract thinking.

We can thus see how Vygotsky's work with blind, deaf-mute and mentally impaired children provided him with the contours of several of the essential ideas of his later cultural-historical theory. Over the centuries cultures develop certain cultural tools that become essential for education and for access to what is called higher culture. These tools are suited to the great majority of people but prove inaccessible for selected groups. These minority groups then suffer the great danger of not getting access to what is considered the cultural heritage or treasure of a certain culture. In other words, they run the danger of remaining at what is considered to be a lower level of cultural development. By analogy with people from so-called primitive societies these children might be called primitive.[10] Implicit in Vygotsky's account are notions about what it is that we call culture, what it is to develop intellectually and what we might understand by the notion of a cultural tool. In the following years, Vygotsky elaborated these notions in what would be called his cultural-historical theory of the higher psychological functions.

Signs and Culture

Vygotsky's notion of culture can be seen as deriving from a synthesis of different strands of thinking. On the one hand, he was inspired by the writings of such Russian scholars as Alexander Potebnya and Gustav Shpet, who stood in a tradition that goes back to the linguist and philosopher Wilhelm von Humboldt. This was a tradition that defended a semiotic conception of culture. On the other hand, Vygotsky took his inspiration from Marxist thinkers who were inclined to regard culture and cultural change in terms of tools, technology and social progress (cf. Van der Veer 1996a; 1996b).

Potebnya and Shpet figured prominently in Vygotsky's writings. Alexander Potebnya defended the view that articulate speech not only serves as a means of communication but shapes our whole way of thinking. In his view, the language we are born into is by far the most important part of our cultural and biological heritage. Without verbal concepts no science would have been possible and without words humans would have remained savages, because words are 'the first and fundamental means of progress' (Potebnya 1926/1989, pp. 197–8). In Potebnya's view (based on that of Von Humboldt), words served at least three functions: (1) they make one's private ideas accessible, because these have to be stated in the conventional terms of some language; (2) for the same reason one's ideas become less idiosyncratic; (3) once formulated, one's private ideas become objectively available. In that external form they exert a certain influence on the language users themselves. As Potebnya (1926/1989, p. 127) put it, language is not just a means to understand the other but also a means to understand oneself. Gustav Shpet, likewise, in his attempt to define cultural psychology or – as he called it – ethnopsychology, described culture as existing in sign systems. In his words, the subject-matter of cultural psychology 'is understood only through the deciphering and interpretation of these signs. That these signs are not merely features of things but also communications about them is obvious from the fact that the existence of the corresponding things is not confined to the pure phenomenon of things. In other words, we are dealing with signs which do not only refer to things but also express some *meaning*' (Shpet 1927/1989, p. 514). Hence, at the basis of cultural psychology is semiotics, a theory of signs, which enables us to interpret the objective, language-based signs and meanings which the subject experiences in a given culture. Reading Potebnya and Shpet, one arrives at a conception of the human being molded by the language he or she speaks. The classification of the world into different categories, the form our thinking takes, the unique way in which we influence ourselves by speaking, the social origin of consciousness in speech, the conception of human beings as being influenced by the objective signs available in a culture; these were all key ideas of Potebnya's and Shpet's linguistic writings. They were also ideas that, in one form or another, would resurface in Vygotsky's cultural-historical theory of the higher psychological functions.

 A rather different influence on Vygotsky's thinking about culture was that of the prevailing Marxist ideas of his time (which overlapped with much older and contemporary non-Marxist ideas). One key idea was that culture is what makes us into human beings and that fundamental for culture is tool use. Both Marx and Engels had argued that human beings are unique in that they make use of tools. Engels (1925) hypothesized that concerted tool use or labor stimulated the development of language as humans needed to communicate with each other during the labor process. By means of tools and language human beings were able to change their environment and thereby themselves. Thus culture in this view was based on tool use and language and was restricted to humans. Moreover, for many thinkers it followed that cultures reach higher levels as human beings developed more complex tools and more complex languages. To substantiate this view, it was necessary to show that animals have no culture, do not acquire genuine language and lack genuine tool use. Also, one needed to show that so-called primitive peoples possessed a less advanced technology and a less developed language. Countless thinkers, psychologists, ethnologists, linguists, and so on, addressed these issues in the nineteenth and the beginning of the twentieth century. Köhler's (1921) famous experiments with chimpanzees demonstrated that animals can make use of tools. Yerkes (1916; 1925; Yerkes and Learned 1925) and others suggested that apes could speak and tried to teach them to do so. After many replication studies and much theoretical reflection the consensus in the 1930s was that animals show no genuine language use, and that insofar as they use tools, the tool of language usage plays no significant role in their lives whatsoever. In his repeated discussions of the investigations of Köhler and others, Vygotsky (1929a; 1930) reached essentially the same conclusion. Thus, in his view the essence of the human–animal distinction as defined by the Marxists and others was corroborated.[11]

Comparing Cultures

The historical claim that the development of technology and culture at large go together, and that western civilization has reached ever further stages of development, led almost naturally to the view that contemporary non-western peoples with less advanced technology showed a less advanced culture. In fact, comparing and rank ordering human cultures became a favorite pastime in the nineteenth and early twentieth century (Jahoda 1999). Almost invariably, it was found that the cultural products of 'primitive' people lacked sophistication, that their language lacked abstract terms and that their mentality was child-like, magical, emotional, irrational, and so on. Having studied countless books about 'primitive' language, art, religion, folklore, and so on, the famous French armchair ethnographer Lucien Lévy-Bruhl (1910/1922; 1922/1976; 1949; 1966; 1975) contrasted the western mentality with what he called the 'pre-logical' thinking of non-western cultures. The very term 'pre-logical' already suggested that non-western people had yet to reach the western level of thinking. Unfortunately, it is very difficult to reach conclusions about persons' mentality or intellect on the basis of, say, their language. Does a paucity of color names in a language reflect limited color vision of its speakers? It does not. Does the fact that French nouns have genders make the French language less abstract than English? Certainly not. As contemporary and later critics pointed out, much of the thinking of Lévy-Bruhl and others was circular: proceeding from the assumption that non-western people were primitive they found their language, memory, mentality, etc. to be primitive, which in turn confirmed their original assumption (Evans-Pritchard 1934; Jahoda 1999; Leroy 1927; Thurnwald 1928; Van der Veer 2003).

The German psychologist Heinz Werner also paid a lot of attention to the comparison of cultures and ran into similar problems. Werner's books abounded with statements about the alleged levels of cultures. He spoke, for example, about our western 'advanced spiritual existence', 'heightened mental habitus', 'spiritual superiority' (Werner 1924, pp. 3–4), and about western 'advanced cultural man' (Werner 1926, p. 99), whom he contrasted with the 'lower races' (ibid., p. 42) and the 'poorest types of pygmoid tribes' (Werner 1931, p. 86). Werner's writings typically followed the same pattern: he outlined the developmental stages (from more primitive to less primitive) of some capacity, say the ability to write poems using rhythm, rhyme and alliteration, and then showed that the most primitive stage in poem writing was characteristic of the most primitive society, the more advanced lyrics characteristic of more advanced societies and so on. Nowhere, however, did Werner explain how he arrived at his global assessments of cultures as a whole – say, that North-American Indians are less primitive than Australian aborigines or African Bushmen. And this posed a serious problem for his thinking, because unless the judgment about a specific capacity and the assessment of the level of a specific culture are independent, statements such as 'in primitive society x the level of poetry is primitive' become completely tautological. However, rank ordering societies would involve assessing the poetry, prose, dance, religion, morals, art, technology, social structure, laws, etc. of various societies according to some debatable standards and then arriving at global qualitative or quantitative conclusions concerning the relative 'value' or 'level' of these societies. But what standards could that be? In what sense is monotheism more advanced than polytheism? And shamanism on a higher level than spiritism? And given that one could reach consensus concerning one particular cultural phenomenon, how would one come to global assessments of cultures as a whole, let alone compare them in meaningful ways? (cf. Van der Veer 1996a; 1996b).

I have mentioned Lévy-Bruhl and Werner because they (together with Thurnwald, cf. Van der Veer and Valsiner 1991) formed an important source of inspiration for Vygotsky's thinking about culture and the comparison of cultures. Just like Lévy-Bruhl and Werner, Vygotsky was inclined to speak of cultures as being of a lower or higher quality. Speaking about the Islamic culture in Uzbekistan, for example, he claimed that their culture was 'low' or 'backward' and that the Uzbeks still had to 'take a grandiose leap on the ladder of cultural development' (Vygotsky 1929b). Given that one cannot meaningfully rank order cultures as a whole, these were ethnocentric labels and claims, I think. Of course, when Vygotsky made these claims he was probably not thinking of morals, religion and so on, but of the extent to which a society promotes the access to and development of rational scientific thinking through appropriate schooling. If I understand him well, he considered those societies to be backward that had not developed the scientific mode of thought or barred access to scientific thinking for certain groups, such as women. And, quite probably, he regarded societies that used enculturation strategies other than the modern western school (e.g. rote learning) as inferior as well. Whether this is ethnocentrism remains to be seen. But it certainly seemed so in the Soviet Union of the 1930s, as we will see in Chapter 5.

It is one thing to be mildly ethnocentric; it is quite another thing to be racist. To get a proper perspective on Vygotsky's thinking, we should realize that around the 1920s many scientists still believed that persons of non-western cultures represented other, and decidedly inferior, races. Scholars such as Cyril Burt, Louis Terman and Robert Yerkes believed that the putatively inferior achievements of people from other cultures could be explained on biological grounds (Gould 1981). The alleged lack of intelligence of Australian aborigines and African Negroes was due to their genes. It was here that Vygotsky, consistent with his thinking about cultural tools and signs, advocated a radically different view. Drawing on the work of the German ethnographer Richard Thurnwald (1922; 1928; 1938; cf. Melk-Koch 1989), he claimed that there are no relevant genetic differences whatsoever between the different human groups – whether yellow, brown, red, or white – currently living on our globe. That viewpoint implied that if we find differences in cognitive functioning between different ethnic groups these differences should be attributed to cultural factors. It implied, more specifically, that if Australian aborigines all failed a Western intelligence test, this failure should not be attributed to their inherent stupidity but to a lack of formal training. In other words, these aborigines probably lacked the specific cultural tools that would enable them to solve the western-type intellectual problems. In that particular sense, we might say that the aborigines were intellectually 'primitive'. Just like the children discussed by Petrova (1925), the aborigines were not feeble-minded, but lacked a specific training. With proper training (read: the western-type of schooling) they would gradually reach our level of intellectual functioning. In fine, Vygotsky claimed that subjects from non-western cultures functioned on an intellectually inferior level, but were by no means inherently incapable of reaching our level of thinking. In the 1920s, when eugenic societies still flourished and the USA used immigration quotas for different ethnic groups on the assumption that they were genetically inferior (Gould 1981), this was a radical viewpoint. And it would still take many decades before scholars would take an even more radical step by stating that not only is there no difference in the genetic make-up of different ethnic groups, but neither can we uphold the idea that modes of thinking in one ethnic group are superior to those of another. Just like in biology, where the idea that different species cannot be rank ordered on some scale of ascending superiority arrived late, psychology was slow to embrace the idea that west is not always best.

Cultural Tools and Mediated Performance: An Example

What was Vygotsky thinking of when he asserted that certain cultures are more advanced than others? What cultural tools did he have in mind? And how do cultural tools allow us to think differently or better? To clarify these issues, I will first discuss an empirical investigation that illustrated the use of cultural tools in a task that required sustained attention and memory. The investigation was carried out by Vygotsky's collaborator Aleksey Leontiev in 1931. Leontiev presented his subjects with a well-known task: they were asked 18 questions, seven of which concerned the color of things. Subjects were encouraged to answer promptly and with one word. However, in each 'game' of 18 questions Leontiev specified two colors that were 'forbidden'. Also, the subjects were never to repeat a color. Leontiev's particular interest was in the subjects' ability to make use of cultural tools to solve a task of this sort. To investigate this ability, he supplied the subjects with a rather primitive cultural tool, namely a set of colored cards (Leontiev 1931; 1932). The idea was that if, for example, 'blue' and 'red' were the forbidden colors, the subjects might use the red and blue cards to aid their performance. One strategy would be to turn cards upside down that were forbidden or had already been mentioned. Naturally, one would expect that younger subjects have more difficulties with the forbidden colors game than adults. But what did Leontiev actually find? First of all, he found that faultless performance was beyond most children and adults when no colored cards were supplied (Van der Veer 1994). However, when colored cards were given to subjects of different age groups an interesting picture evolved. The youngest children, who were five to six years old, proved unable to make any intelligent use of the cards. That is, they might manipulate them, but not in a sensible way, and, in fact, the introduction of the cards did not diminish their number of errors in the game. For older children the colored cards did make a difference: for both the eight- to nine-year-old and the ten- to thirteen-year-old children performance with cards was much better than in the no-card condition. The children evidently profited from the presence of the cards by turning them upside down and so on. However, the most striking result was found for adults: they made very few errors, but their performance was not improved by the introduction of the cards. What happened? On closer inspection, Leontiev found that adults hardly made use of the colored cards at all. Evidently, they relied on other means than the cards to prevent errors.

Leontiev's explanation of his set of findings seemed intuitively plausible. In his view, the youngest children could not manage this complicated task, because they were still incapable of making use of the cultural tools supplied. In a way, then, Leontiev felt he was measuring their natural attention span or memory capacity, unaided by cultural instruments. The older children obviously grasped how to make efficient use of the cards and enhanced their performance accordingly. Finally, the adults no longer made use of the colored cards, but unlike the youngest children they did not rely on their 'natural' memory or attention. Rather, Leontiev suggested, they had switched to internal means and strategies. Presumably, adults can make use of powerful verbal means to avoid making mistakes in this specific task (e.g. by answering 'azure' when 'blue' was the forbidden color) and no longer need such crude external cultural tools as the colored cards.

Now, the interesting thing is that Vygotsky and his colleagues took the findings of Leontiev to be a model for normal human ontogenetic development. That is, they speculated that in human ontogeny there is, first, a stage of natural performance, when subjects are not yet capable of using the available cultural means; second, a stage of external tool use, when subjects overwhelmingly rely on the available external cultural means; and, finally, a third stage of internal mediation. In other words, up from a certain age mental functioning is almost entirely mediated, that is, comes about with the help of either external or internal cultural means. During ontogeny most external means are replaced by internal means. To argue this view further, Vygotsky came up with a variety of examples from child psychology and cultural anthropology. He noticed, for example, that children who learn to count prefer to make use of body parts, such as fingers, to assist their counting. It takes some time before they can count mentally. Historically speaking, one can see that in many cultures counting is based on the decimal system, presumably because we have ten fingers. Or take the example of arithmetic. Most children learn to do arithmetic by making use of paper and pencil and certain conventional graphic representations. It is only gradually that they learn to do arithmetic by heart using the same or other conventions. Another example is that of remembering a specific task, say, of making a phone call or buying something at the grocery shop. Young children are particularly prone to forget such things but can help themselves by tying a knot in their handkerchief. This external sign helps them to take appropriate action. Again, we can find similar procedures in the anthropological literature: in many cultures adults have been found to remember things by tying knots in strings or making carvings in wood. To Vygotsky these examples proved that many cultures have developed means to make complex mental processes possible and that children within each culture have to learn these anew. Moreover, he argued that in both human history[12] and ontogeny the use of material means precedes that of verbal means. Of course, as adults we still use material means such as notebooks, index cards and so on, but nevertheless we have learned to do many things by heart. What this means is that we have switched from one cultural tool to another, namely from counting using body parts to counting using audible or silent speech. That brings us to that most powerful cultural tool of human beings: human language or speech.

Verbal Signs

Naturally, colored cards are not very efficient cultural tools; they can only be used fruitfully in a very limited number of tasks. Human language is a much more flexible instrument. Take the example of memorizing a shopping list. An efficient strategy to remember what items to buy is to divide them into different categories: vegetables, dairy products, meat products, and so on. This procedure, known as chunking, improves memory performance greatly. Apparently, by using the cultural tool of grouping different objects under joint labels we can improve our 'natural' memory. What difference does language make in complex mental performance? What functions does language have? How should we conceive of the acquisition and development of language in human ontogeny? These were key questions for Vygotsky in his theorizing to which we shall now turn.

There is no doubt that Vygotsky considered language to be the greatest cultural tool ever invented. Vygotsky believed that the whole human mind is constructed and changed by the acquisition of speech and, much later, specific verbal concepts. The original function of speech is communication: children and adults use speech to express emotions and to communicate about the world. Using speech, parents draw attention to salient features of the environment, introduce certain ways to see the world (e.g. by distinguishing between 'dogs' and 'cats', and 'cars' and 'buses'), and guide their children through complex tasks. Gradually the child is introduced to an environment that is segmented by words into different objects, categories, and so on, and gradually the child learns to tackle problems making use of speech. Take the example of laying a jigsaw puzzle (cf. Wertsch 1981). At first jigsaw puzzles are beyond the capacity of young children, and parents typically verbally guide their child through this complex task. Parents tell their child, for example, to begin the jigsaw puzzle in the corners, or to first gather all pieces of a specific color. The completion of the puzzle is a joint performance, where the youngest children most of the time simply carry out the verbal instructions of the parent. It is only gradually that the responsibility for task completion is shifted from the parent to the child. Typically, children learn to guide themselves through the problem-solving process by giving themselves verbal instructions. Thus, children will say aloud to themselves that they will first search for the red pieces, then switch to the blue ones and so on. In a way, then, they are now guiding themselves through the process just like they were earlier being guided by their parents. This shift from other-regulation to self-regulation, as it has been called, is heavily language-based. Finally, still older or more skilled children will solve the jigsaw puzzle by giving themselves tacit instructions, by thinking about the respective problem-solving steps to make. In Vygotsky's own words:

> The mother draws the child's attention to something. The child follows the instructions and pays attention to what she points out. Here we always have two separate functions. Then the child begins to direct his attention himself, plays the role of the mother vis-à-vis himself. He develops a complex system of functions that were originally shared. One person orders, the other carries out. Man orders and obeys himself.
> (Vygotsky 1930/1997, p. 96)

In a way, then, we see a process similar to that of the use of the cultural means in the forbidden colors task: first the usage is visible or audible, and then it goes underground, so to speak. We can no longer see that adults use speech to solve problems, to plan their actions, and so on, but we know it through introspection. We know our thinking is largely verbal thinking. Vygotsky described this whole process in various ways. First, he observed that the introduction of speech changes our way of thinking. Second, he discussed how speech changes from social speech via egocentric speech to inner speech. Third, he emphasized that speech is introduced in social interaction. In the next paragraphs I will discuss these different viewpoints on the introduction of speech.

Vygotsky noted that children are no mindless beings before they acquire speech. Infants can remember and recognize faces, can search for objects, can imitate movements, and so on. This shows that there is mental functioning before speech, or what Vygotsky called preverbal thought.[13] Also, there is speech that serves no obvious function, such as babbling. However, at a certain moment in the child's development, thinking and speech merge and the child becomes capable of verbal thought. The child is now capable of directing its own thinking processes when laying jigsaw puzzles, for example. Vygotsky argued that this is important, because the child is now capable of sustained, concentrated effort and is less easily distracted by environmental stimuli. Also, the introduction of speech creates a 'semantic field', a field of meanings: as said above, the environment is structured by the terms and meanings that the child acquires with speech. So, one way of looking at the acquisition of full-fledged speech is to say that two lines of development, those of pre-verbal thinking and pre-cognitive speech, merge to create the uniquely human product of verbal thinking.

With Piaget, Vygotsky observed that children often talk out loud without seeming to address someone. His interpretation of this phenomenon, called 'egocentric speech' by Piaget, was a developmental one. Before children become capable of tacit thinking, they need to give themselves instructions in audible speech. This explains why young children often resort to 'egocentric' speech when they are confronted with a problem. The child states the problem, whether there is a solution, and what to do next. Egocentric speech, then, is an intermediate stage between the social, interactive speech of adult–child conversations and the 'underground' stage of genuine, private thinking. Its function is to guide the child through a problematic situation. Ultimately, this viewpoint implies that rational thought originates in the conversations of the child with adults or more able peers.

Finally, this whole view of the acquisition of speech implies that all higher mental processes originate in social interaction. It is while solving a practical problem that adults or more advanced peers introduce cultural tools such as language to the child. The child can subsequently master these tools and guide its own behavior in situations that would otherwise be difficult to handle. Individual skills can thus be seen to depend on the acquisition of cultural tools in social interaction (cf. Balamore and Wozniak 1999; Wozniak 1999).

Lower and Higher Psychological Processes

We are now in a position to state the basic outlines of Vygotsky's cultural-historical theory. The theory states that cultures develop cultural tools to solve specific problems. These cultural tools, among which language is by far the most important one, are acquired by all normal children living in such a culture. Language is acquired in social interaction and transforms the child's behavior. Through language, children can increasingly steer their own behavior and solve complex problems. The mastering of cultural tools proceeds through different stages and is characterized by a global transition from external mediation, or tool use, to internal mediation. Assuming that different contemporary non-western cultures are similar to historical cultures that have now disappeared, we may surmise, on the basis of cultural anthropological evidence, that the transition from external to internal mediation took place in human history as well. It is crucial that cultural tools are mastered as they represent the highest achievements of humankind. Thus, children who do not learn to read or write have no access to much of human culture. Children who do not acquire speech (e.g. deaf-mutes) are in the desperate position that they cannot develop verbal thinking. We must do everything within our possibilities to guarantee such children access to our culture by developing other cultural tools.

Now, this whole theory seems to deny individual differences. It seems to deny that some children are inherently brighter than others. It seems to ignore the fact that much of human development is dependent on maturational factors, on the growth of the brain, the myelinization of nerve fibers, the secretion of hormones, and so on. Or does it? What was Vygotsky's position regarding these issues? Was he really an environmentalist who ignored the genetic equipment of children and the role of maturation in development? Well, first of all, through his work with physically and mentally impaired children, Vygotsky was perfectly aware that some of us are less equipped to begin the enculturation process than others (see above). He was also aware of and wrote about the existence of particularly gifted children. He knew perfectly well about differences in innate abilities. However, his theory was about the interlocking of nature and nurture, about the way innate potential is channeled and changed by culture in all subjects. And it was about the emancipation of disadvantaged children. In this connection, it is necessary to pay attention to the distinction Vygotsky made between lower and higher psychological processes. In Vygotsky's view infants come well equipped to this world: they dispose of a variety of initial reflexes (e.g. grasping, rooting, sucking), they can visually scan outlines of patterns, they recognize faces, they have a well-developed sense of smell, they are finely tuned to the sound categories and rhythms of human language, and so on (Cole and Cole 1996). Vygotsky called such abilities lower or natural psychological processes.

They are 'lower' in the sense of being less complex than 'higher' abilities such as chess playing, which require considerable training, a vast memory, and so on. They may be termed 'natural', because they are independent of culture and historical period. Throughout human history, children in all cultures presumably displayed the same basic repertoire of reflexes. As Vygotsky said:

> We have no reason to assume that the human brain underwent an essential biological evolution in the course of human history. We have no reason to assume that the brain of primitive man differed from our brain, was an inferior brain, or had a biological structure different from ours ... The biological evolution of man was finished before the beginning of his historical development. And it would be a flagrant mixing up of the concepts of biological evolution and historical development to try to explain the difference between our thinking and the thinking of primitive man by claiming that primitive man stands on another level of biological development.
> (Vygotsky 1930/1997, p. 97)[14]

Equipped with this basic set of abilities the neonate commences to interact with his environment and it is now that culture becomes utterly relevant.

Of course, some functions will continue to develop with relatively minor input from the cultural environment. Thus, visual acuity, speed of reactions and locomotion will develop even with minimal interference from the socio-cultural environment. Also, it is possible that some form of improvement of the memory capacity would take place even when a child was raised in relative isolation. In this sense, we may speak with Vygotsky of a hypothetical natural line of development in ontogeny. Naturally, we have no way of investigating this line as we cannot separate a child from his or her environment for ethical reasons, and the few sad cases of children who have been raised in isolation prove very little.

Now, there exist a vast number of ways in which cultural traditions co-determine and shape child development. Cultures vary in their sleeping arrangements, sleeping schedules, food patterns, qualities they prefer in children, socialization strategies, and so on. Of all this tremendous variety, Vygotsky was primarily interested in the way culture shapes our cognitive, intellectual functioning through semiotic means. When he spoke of higher mental processes, he had in mind mental processes that were reshaped by the acquisition of language and language-based means such as categorizing. In this sense, he could speak of lower and higher perception, lower and higher attention, and natural and higher, or logical memory. I shall illustrate this latter distinction by way of an example. Suppose that a child is required to memorize a list of unconnected words such as: table, spoon, tulip, fork, chair, rose, pan, bed, aster, knife, daisy, cupboard. Then it will help enormously to realize that these 12 words can be divided into three categories, namely 'furniture' (table, chair, bed, cupboard), 'kitchen utensils' (spoon, fork, pan, knife), and 'flowers' (tulip, rose, aster, daisy). In other words, we may approach this task in a naïve way and just try to pump the words into our head by simply rehearsing them endlessly in the specified order, or we can resort to the clever cultural device of dividing them into categories and then use these categories to fish out the words from our memory. Using the latter trick will greatly facilitate the memory process. Vygotsky reasoned that young children are less equipped to solve such memory tasks than adults, who are, in their turn, less equipped than memory artists, who make use of even more powerful mnemonics. In that sense, we might describe the child's memory as more 'natural'. In another sense, the child's memory is thoroughly cultural, of course, as it is clearly a verbal and, possibly, a well-trained memory. The important thing to realize is that one and the same task can be solved by a variety of cultural means and that cognitive development can be viewed as the consecutive acquisition of increasingly powerful cultural means. In this context, Vygotsky and his collaborators also used the term 'rearmament':

> In the process of development, the child not only matures, but also becomes rearmed. Precisely this 'rearmament' causes the greatest development and change that we can observe in the child as he transforms into a cultural adult.
>
> (Vygotsky and Luria 1993, p. 188)

The developing child increases its repertoire of cultural tools by discarding or retaining older tools and learning new ones. As adults we do not notice this simple fact, because so many complex cognitive operations seem to come naturally to us. When multiplying 7 times 15, we no longer notice that we are using an algorithm that we once took a long time to practice and understand, and that we at first could only execute in the material, paper-and-pencil form.

Summarizing, we might say that Vygotsky acknowledged that children are born with certain innate abilities that co-determine their potential for mental development. These capacities he termed lower natural mental processes. A child's actual mental development will depend in part on these natural capacities and their further maturation, but, more importantly, on the cultural tools offered to the child and the way these tools are geared to the child's abilities. A blind child not introduced to the Braille script will remain illiterate, which will seriously hinder his or her intellectual development. A child who is not taught the principles of scientific reasoning will have a hard time discovering these principles him or herself and will likewise be restrained in intellectual development. Finally, such factors as brain development do play a role in mental development, but not in a simple deterministic and unidirectional way. Unlike several of his contemporaries, Vygotsky believed that the structure and functioning of the brain is co-determined by environmental factors, notably the acquisition of speech. He argued that the specifically human way of cognitive functioning that is based on language creates a typically human, dynamic and systemic structure of mind and brain.[15]

The Dynamic and Systemic Nature of Mind and Brain

Let us first discuss the dynamic nature of mind and brain, i.e. the view that both mind and brain change over the course of a human life. That the mind changes during ontogeny was generally accepted, but that the brain may change after a first period of maturation was certainly an original view in the early twentieth century. Vygotsky believed with Heinz Werner that development implies differentiation, articulation and hierarchization (Van der Veer 2004). That is, as the infant grows older, the mental functions become differentiated and more articulate and end up in a hierarchical organization. When infants get excited, for instance, they will both move their arms and legs, and smile, and vocalize. Perception and action are one and the same thing. For adults the picture is very different: they may be very angry and still not show it in any way. Emotion and its behavioral expression have become separated. Thought dominates over motor behavior. Viewing is no longer equivalent to acting. One way to look at these developmental changes is to say with Werner and Vygotsky that mental processes that were originally united have become separated and hierarchically organized. If there is some truth to these claims, then this must mean that mental development is not just a process of organic growth or maturation, but also of dynamic reorganization. Our capacity to retain memory traces may become stronger, our visual acuity may grow, our ability to make delicate movements may increase, but the most important thing is that all these processes can become transformed and organized in a specific way under the influence of verbal thinking.

Such a view has clear repercussions for our thinking about brain organization as well. The brain cannot be a static structure that remains virtually the same during our whole life. We must accept a dynamic view of the brain. And if we accept that view, then we should conceive the dynamic changes not just in terms of growth but in terms of systemic changes. What changes in development is not 'a change within each function. What is changed is chiefly the original link between these functions' (Vygotsky 1930/1997, p. 92). So, the brain is a dynamic, flexible structure that undergoes systemic changes under the influence of the cultural environment. The brain does not deterministically rule our actions and mental processes, but is also shaped by them.[16]

Let us take a simple, and no doubt simplified, example to illustrate the dynamic and systemic structure of the brain. When we see an object, such as a pan, different brain centers will be activated simultaneously. With adults who have handled pans frequently, the visual centers, the olfactory center, the auditory center, the sensory center and the language centers will be activated simultaneously when

```
              ──▶  Smell
                  ╱ ▲  ▲
                 ╱   ╲  ╲
PAN  ──▶  Visual Image ◀──▶ Name
                 ╲   ╱  ╱
                  ╲ ▼  ▼
              ──▶  Touch
```

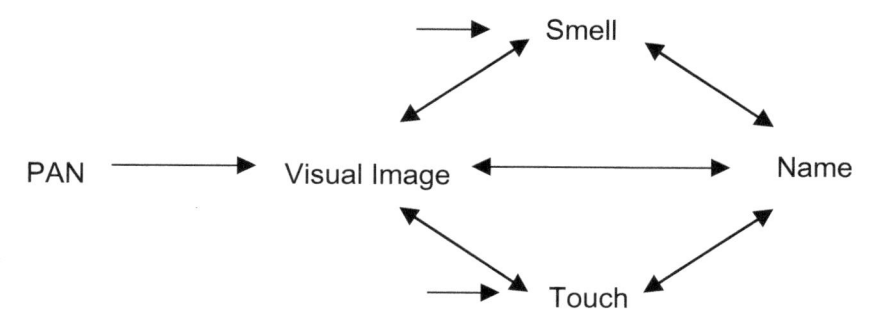

Figure 3.1 A simplified hypothetical brain system

perceiving a pan. This is because we have both seen pans, smelled their metal, heard their sound when they fell or bumped into each other, felt their surface, and learned that they are called pans. Now, we know that these various 'centers' are located in different parts of the brain. The primary visual center is located in the occipital lobe, other visual centers in the temporal lobe, the sensory 'center' in the parietal lobe, and so on. And all these different centers must be somehow connected through different pathways to form specific circuits. Otherwise, the visual image of a pan could not lead to, say, the memory of the word 'pan'. Nor could the smell of an object evoke its visual image. For young children, the picture must be somewhat different. After all, they may have seen pans and perhaps have learned their names, but they almost certainly will not have handled them. That implies that the system of brain centers involved in perceiving pans is different than in adults. Now, Vygotsky's dynamic brain view in its simplest form says just that: mental development results in or is equivalent to shifting systemic relationships between different brain centers (see Figure 3.1).

One advantage of the systemic view is that it allows us to overcome two older views on the localization of mental processes in the brain. The first view, holism, posited that the brain as a whole is responsible for each and every function. This was the view defended by Lashley (1950) in his famous article 'In search of the engram'. The second view was that of strict localizationism, which stated that mental functions are taken care of by strictly localized corresponding brain

```
              → Smell ←
           ↗    ↕      ↘ b
ROSE → Visual image ←──┤ a ├──→ Name
           ↘    ↕      ↗
              → Touch ← c
```

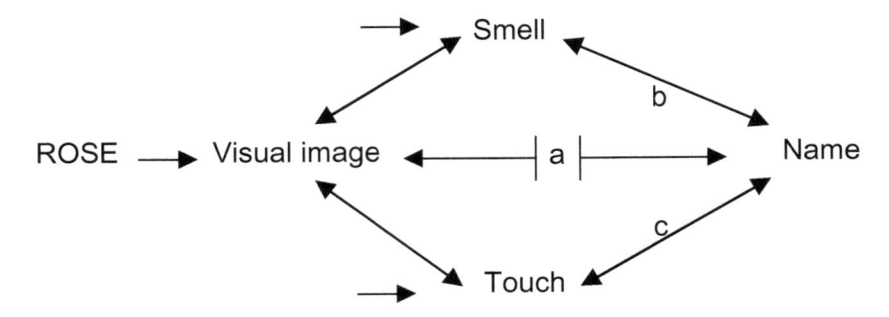

Figure 3.2 A hypothetical example of compensation through systemic relationships

centers. That view was defended by, among others, the phrenologists. Neither view proved correct and we now believe that most mental functions are taken care of by various centers connected through neural pathways.

The second advantage of the systemic view is that it offers a hypothetical explanation for the phenomenon of compensation in cases of brain damage. Take, for example, a case described by Sacks (1985). One of his patients could no longer recognize faces or objects, although he could give a perfect description of them. Shown a glove, he described it as 'a continuous surface unfolded on itself with five outpouchings' (Sacks 1985, p. 13). Shown a rose, he commented that it was 'a convoluted red form with a linear green attachment' that might be 'an inflorescence or flower' (ibid., p. 12). When allowed to smell the rose, however, he immediately identified it as a rose. And when allowed to touch the glove, he identified it as a glove. One way to interpret such findings is in terms of the hypothetical brain systems described above. The idea would be that the nervous pathway from the visual centers that process the visual image to the language centers that contain the name of the object have been damaged or blocked but that recognition is still possible via another route, e.g. via the pathway that leads from the olfactory (smell) 'image' of the object to the center that retains its name. In other words, although the route 'a' from the visual image to the name has been blocked, production of the object's name is still possible through the route 'b' that leads from the olfactory representation of the object to its name, 'rose' (see Figure 3.2).

Such roundabout ways to maintain achievement of a certain mental performance when suffering from brain damage have repeatedly been described by Vygotsky and even more frequently by Luria. However, their focus was more on the usage of higher processes, such as language, to achieve processes that no longer run automatically. An example they repeatedly discussed was that of patients suffering from Parkinson's disease. Such patients may no longer be able to initiate voluntary movements such as walking. They seem to be 'frozen' as it were. However, patients may still be able to walk by introducing compensatory means. One way to do that is by laying pieces of paper on the floor with gaps of about one step between each piece. Patients are now capable of walking by stepping on the pieces of paper (Vygotsky 1930/1997, p. 105). Another example was given by Sacks in his fascinating book *Awakenings*.

> This patient . . . had long since found that she could scarcely start, or stop, or change her direction of motion; that once she had been set in motion, she had no control. It was therefore necessary for her to plan all her motions in advance, with great precision. Thus, moving from her armchair to her divan-bed . . . could never be done *directly* – Miss T. would immediately be 'frozen' in transit, and perhaps stay frozen for half an hour or more. She therefore had to embark on one of two courses of action: in either case, she would rise to her feet, arrange her angle of direction exactly, and shout 'Now!', whereupon she would break into an incontinent run, which could be neither stopped nor changed in direction . . . all paths and trajectories [were] pre-computed and compared, contingency plans and 'fail-safes' prepared in advance. A good deal of Miss T.'s life, in short, was dependent on conscious taking-care and elaborate calculation – but that was the only way she could maintain her existence.
>
> (Sacks 1982, p. 316, n. 21)

How can we explain that such patients can no longer perform certain actions *directly* or automatically, but can find other ways to keep functioning in a more or less adequate manner? Vygotsky believed that the key to the explanation lies in the fact that they resort to external signs to influence their own behavior. The patient as it were influences him or herself from the outside. Vygotsky stated that 'The Parkinsonian patient establishes a connection between different points of his brain through a sign, influencing himself from the periphery' (Vygotsky 1930/1997, p. 106). In other words, both the pieces of paper on the floor and the shouted word 'Now!' are external signs that the patient utilizes to perform actions that he or she can no longer perform automatically. It is as if the patient through an external sign is connecting two parts of the brain that are no longer connected internally. Consequently, the patients' problems are solved by resorting to an ontogenetically prior *modus operandi*, that of external mediation (cf. Luria 1932b).

In the final years of his career, Vygotsky (e.g. 1934/1977; 1935) attempted to formulate a number of general laws for the dynamic shifts that the brain systems responsible for certain mental processes undergo during ontogeny. He also realized that, if we take the dynamic and systemic viewpoint seriously, we should expect one and the same brain lesion to have different psychological effects at different age levels. The three general laws for the dynamic shifts in brain regulation are as follows (Vygotsky 1935):

(1) The law of progression upwards, i.e. processes that were first taken care of by lower centers are later taken care of by higher centers. Here Vygotsky mentioned that some behaviors are first taken care of by reflexes and later become voluntary. For example, grasping in infancy is first based on the grasping reflex, but after three to four months this reflex is replaced by voluntary grasping.
(2) The law of subordination, i.e. after the move upwards the lower centers remain functioning, but under the control of higher centers. The intervention of the higher centers makes the psychological process more complex and flexible.
(3) The law of regression, i.e. if for some reason the higher centers are damaged the lower centers may regain their independency and take care of the psychological process.

Vygotsky realized that these so-called laws were no more than rules of thumb that only partially reflected the complex and dynamic character of the brain regulation of psychological processes. He added, for example, that regression shouldn't be taken literally: in no sense does the adult patient become child-like again. Although in both cases a higher center may not be operative, this is for different reasons. Immature centers in the child and damaged centers in the adult may produce comparable symptoms but, dynamically speaking, they resemble each other as two trains 'going into opposite directions' (Vygotsky 1935, p. 123). Vygotsky also remarked that the third law, the law of regression, does not always hold. In certain cases, when a brain center is damaged a *higher* center may take over. The examples given above illustrate this possibility. For example, the Parkinson patient who can no longer walk automatically (a process presumably guided by lower subcortical centers) can walk by resort to conscious, deliberate walking through speech (a process presumably guided by cortical centers) (Van der Veer and Valsiner 1994).

The laws formulated by Vygotsky are undoubtedly simplistic and only partially correct, but they had certain definitive advantages in comparison to the static views of brain organization prevalent at the time. First, he realized that the brain organization of psychological processes is subject to major changes that have nothing to do with maturation or growth (e.g. the restructuring of brain organization of many psychological processes through the acquisition of language). Second, this dynamic or chronogenic viewpoint allowed him to understand the fact that the impact of brain damage depends on the patient's age. To give a trivial example: an infant struck with deafness will not automatically acquire speech; an adult struck with deafness may retain his speech abilities. Third, Vygotsky realized that many psychological processes are taken care of by complex systems of hierarchically organized brain centers. Fourth, this viewpoint allowed him to understand how and why compensation is frequently possible in patients suffering from neurological damage. Vygotsky's collaborator Luria investigated these matters in great detail and made major contributions to the new field of neuropsychology. Finally, these principles imply that the organization of mind and brain is ultimately dependent upon age, personal experience, training, and the acquisition of cultural tools such as language. Mind and brain are crucially influenced by culture.

Conclusions

In this chapter we have outlined the principles of what was to be called the cultural-historical theory of higher psychological processes. As its name suggests, this theory stated that higher mental processes are culturally and historically variable. Human mental development is inextricably tied to the mastering of cultural tools that tend to be different in different historical periods. The mastering of cultural tools, notably that of speech, allows human beings to master themselves, to be capable of foresight, to make plans, to have self-control. In that process the original natural (lower) processes become transformed into higher processes. Because the human mind is so fundamentally culturally determined we may expect cognitive differences between people from different cultures. Also, we may expect the mastering of cultural tools to lead to different organizations of the brain. The organization of both mind and brain changes over time and is dependent on age, training, education and diseases. A systemic dynamic view of the mind-brain system allows us to understand the crucial role of age in pathology and the phenomena of compensation. The crucial idea of the cultural-historical theory is that in order to understand the human mind we have to step outside of it and to look at the cultural artifacts human beings have created.

The cultural-historical theory was created over a period of about five years, beginning in approximately 1927. In the final years of his life Vygotsky returned to the issue of education and its relation to mental development. What kind of education do we need? What kind of cultural tools do we want our children to master? Are the cultural differences in cognitive functioning that one finds caused by specific tools or by schooling? And do cultural tools, once mastered, remain stable over time? These were some of the questions Vygotsky and his collaborators struggled with and tried to answer within the framework of cultural-historical theory. In the next chapter we will see which provisional answers Vygotsky had reached by the end of his career.

Chapter 4

The Zone of Proximal Development

Intelligence Testing in the Soviet Union

When Binet and his colleague Simon developed a simple series of questions to find out which school children deserved the teacher's special attention they could not foresee that this would result in enormous changes both within the science of psychology and in society at large (Binet and Simon 1905). Soon leading psychologists all over the world were busy discussing and applying Binet and Simon's test and developing mental tests of their own. Burt in England, Stern in Germany and Goddard, Terman, Thurstone and Yerkes in the United States belonged to the many researchers who developed the practice and theory of intelligence testing further. With surprising speed mental tests spread over the world to serve a variety of purposes: not just diagnosis, but selection and prediction as well. In that process much of Binet's original intention was lost. Whereas Binet believed his mental test scores to reflect the child's achievement in tasks similar to those trained at school, many of the new researchers believed that the scores reflected children's innate intelligence. Moreover, that innate intelligence was believed to be more or less immutable and the eugenic movement viewed mental tests as excellent instruments to distinguish between those fit and those unfit for reproduction (Gould 1981). Binet (1911/1973, p. 126) vehemently protested against such 'brutal pessimism', against the idea that 'the intelligence of an individual is a fixed quantity, a quantity we cannot augment', but his words were not heard by everyone and to this very day the debate about the nature of intelligence as measured by IQ tests continues.

Intelligence testing reached its peak in America in the 1910s and 1920s (Boring 1950; Hines 1924; Peterson 1926/1969; Wells 1927).

Such journals as *Journal of Educational Research*, *Journal of Educational Psychology*, *Pedagogical Seminary*, and *British Journal of Psychology* published hundreds of articles on mental testing. Researchers began comparing test scores of different groups of people: e.g. prisoners vs non-prisoners, inhabitants of an asylum vs non-inhabitants, women vs men, blacks vs whites, and so on. Mental tests were used on a massive scale to select people for different functions or jobs. But most tests were administered in connection with education: to fit the instruction to pupils, or, perhaps, to fit pupils to available schools. Terman and his colleagues (Terman et al. 1923) advised to test all school children repeatedly ('What pupils shall be tested? The answer is all!'). Their assumption was that age is an insufficient criterion to compose classrooms. After all, children of the same chronological age may vary greatly in intelligence. To offer these children the same curriculum would be unfair: the bright children will not be intellectually challenged and the poor students may not be able to cope with the program. A better way to proceed, according to Terman (1920) and his colleagues, is to test all children and to put those with the same mental age together. In Terman's (1921, p. 27) words: 'The mentally old and mentally young do not belong together.' Although such ideas met with occasional opposition (e.g. Bishop 1924; Mateer 1918), it is easy to find many articles from that period which deal with the use of IQ tests to improve classroom composition, to construct optimal curricula, to optimize the choice of textbooks, and so on (e.g. Brooks 1922; Fordyce 1921; Kallom 1922; Wilson 1926). IQ scores were often combined or correlated with achievement scores (expressed in an 'achievement quotient' or 'accomplishment quotient') to see whether the child profited optimally from the instruction offered (e.g. Burks 1928; Coy 1930; McCrory 1932; Popenoe 1927; Torgerson 1922; Wilson 1928). In sum, it was widely discussed whether mental tests could be used to improve the fit between pupil and curriculum and many researchers believed this to be the case.

The situation in the Soviet Union in the 1920s was not essentially different. Many of the leading researchers took an interest in mental tests; journals such as *Pedologiya* and *Psikhofiziologiya Truda i Psikhotekhnika* published many papers on testing; school children's IQs were tested on a massive scale; vocational tests were widely used;

and a society for testologists was founded (Rahmani 1973, p. 54). Just like in the West, some researchers tended to defend the massive use of mental tests (e.g. Blonsky, Lange, Nechaev), or developed tests of their own (e.g. Rossolimo 1926); others had mixed feelings (e.g. Kornilov), and still others were quite critical (Basov, Chelpanov, Krupskaya, Zalkind) (Joravsky 1989). Meanwhile, the massive testing of groups of children led to some remarkable results. First, Russian children in general tended to score lower on the Binet tests than, say, French children. Second, the children of ethnic minorities tended to score lower than Russian children. Third, children of the *intelligentsia* and of rich farmers (*kulaks*) tended to score higher than other children. Fourth, on the basis of their test scores, far too many children were referred to schools for special education. Now, one might react to this pattern of results in many ways. For example, one may accept the results and state they reflect differences in innate ability between these various groups and persons. Or, one may accept the results and state they reflect different cultural backgrounds. Such reasoning may, in its turn, lead to a plea for developing new, culture-fair tests, or for the use of different standards (e.g. admitting children from minorities with less than the required entrance scores to specific schools), or to the development of special programs for specific groups. In fact, all of these reactions were voiced in the Soviet Union of that time (for example, the Russians, as well, had a eugenic society with its own scientific journal; cf. Kurek 2004), but in the end it was the Party that decided what it saw as the proper course to take. Mental tests were increasingly viewed as bourgeois instruments that artificially maintained the age-old class differences. The tests could not possibly reflect innate abilities. After all, there was no reason to assume that Russian children are less gifted than French children. However, pointing to poor cultural environments as an explanation for low test scores also became increasingly unacceptable (Bauer 1952). After all, what could still be wrong with the environment of honest laborers or ethnic minorities after more than ten years of the Soviet regime? The conclusion could be no other than that the test results were misleading and led to unwanted societal results (Rudik 1932). The millions of children of peasants and laborers needed to enter the new educational system and the enthusiasts of mental testing were not allowed to frustrate this process. In 1936, with the Pedology Decree, mental tests became forbidden in the Soviet Union.

The Zone of Proximal Development

Vygotsky had always been quite critical of IQ tests (Vygotsky 1926, p. 331). Working as a clinical psychologist with deaf, blind and mentally impaired children, he was in need of truly diagnostic instruments that allow one to make a prognosis of the child's mental development, or to devise prosthetic means. The apodictic numbers of the Stanford-Binet test seemed of little value in this context. He also vehemently opposed the idea advocated by such researchers as Burt and Terman that mental tests measured pure genetic endowment. However, as said above, the Soviet educational system was confronted with millions of pupils of very diverse economic and cultural backgrounds (e.g. whose parents were illiterate or did not have Russian as their native tongue). It was an issue of great practical significance to find the right educational route for these children. Working at the Herzen Pedagogical Institute in Leningrad, Vygotsky could not ignore the issue. No wonder, then, that Vygotsky attentively followed the publications about the use of mental tests to improve the instruction in schools and to discover hidden talents. No wonder that he was interested in finding or adopting new diagnostic means to predict mental development. And, finally, no wonder that he paid a great deal attention to the general relation between instruction and mental development. It was in searching for an answer to these questions that Vygotsky hit upon the concept of the zone of proximal development (cf. Chaiklin 2003).

As far as we know, Vygotsky first raised the topic of the zone of proximal development in 1933. Several times that year he talked and wrote about the concept. His final mention of the idea is in the sixth chapter of his *Thinking and Speech*, dictated in the spring of 1934 and, all in all, we have only eight published texts where the concept of the zone of proximal development is mentioned or discussed (Vygotsky 1933/1935a; 1933/1935b; 1933/1935c; 1933/1935d; 1933/1935e; 1933/1966; 1933/1984; 1934a). Interestingly, Vygotsky never claimed to have invented the concept. On the contrary, he repeatedly stated that the concept was widely used in the pedological practice of that time and referred to American researchers such as Owell and McCarthy, and to the German educationalist Meumann, as originators of (aspects of) the concept. Unfortunately, these references were so vague that no one has as yet been able to clarify the origin and history of the concept and until the present day the concept of the zone of proximal development is attributed to Vygotsky.

When we look at Vygotsky's statements about the zone of proximal development in chronological order, we can see at once that the concept arose in the context of the practice of intelligence testing and only later acquired a more general character. What was that context? Several researchers (e.g. Burt 1927, p. 178; Meumann 1914, p. 766; Stern 1920, p. 245; Terman et al. 1923, p. 74) had noticed that bright children tended to lose their edge after several years of schooling. That is, on average, children with a high IQ tend to lose IQ points, children with normal IQ tend to be stable, and children with a low IQ tend to gain IQ points. In other words, school seemed to have a leveling effect on intelligence scores[17] (Vygotsky 1933/1935e). Moreover, high-IQ children also profit less from school in terms of newly gained knowledge and skills. Although they may still have the best grades, their relative success in one year of study is lower than that of average or dull children.[18] How should we explain this finding, that bright children apparently profit less from school instruction? The obvious answer is that bright children are not being stimulated enough; they are not sufficiently challenged by the instruction. The instruction that is usual for their chronological age is simply too easy as their mental age is higher than the average. Children learn little from doing tasks that are below their intellectual level. Neither do they learn very much from solving problems that are at exactly their intellectual level. This is a very unfortunate situation, Vygotsky argued, because what instruction should do is exactly the opposite. Instruction should offer tasks that are *above* the child's intellectual level, but not too far above it (see below). That way the child is sufficiently stimulated to try the new problems and to rise above his or her own intellectual level as it were.

If we accept that reasoning, then in school we need to do two things. First, we must carefully establish the individual child's intellectual level. Second, we must establish the range of tasks and problems that are above the child's intellectual level, but not too far above it. It is here that Vygotsky mentioned the new method of measuring children's intellectual potential. Formerly, he said, we measured the child's intellectual level by establishing the number and type of problems the child could solve independently. This gave us an indication of the child's mental age and we tried to adjust the level of instruction to that mental age. However, there is a new method of measuring a child's intellectual level which proceeds by testing the child twice: first, when the child solves the problems independently and then when the child solves the problems together with a more able partner. This second procedure yields a score that proves to be the more revealing one. In Vygotsky's own words:

> I show them [the children] different ways to solve the problem. Various authors and various investigators utilize in various cases various ways to demonstrate the solutions. The children are fully shown how to solve the problem and they are asked to do it again; or the beginning of the problem solving process is shown and the children are asked to finish it, or the children are asked leading questions. In a word, in various ways we ask the child to solve the problem with our help.
> (Vygotsky 1933/1935e, pp. 41–2)

Of course, when we apply this procedure, we will see that children solve more problems with assistance than they would independently. However, the interesting thing is that different children are capable of profiting from the hints and help of others to a different degree. Some children will be able to gain one year of mental age with help, others two or more. In Vygotsky's view, these differences were far from accidental: a child who profits more from the help of a more able partner has more intellectual potential. This is so because the ability to grasp or imitate the actions of the more able partner tells something about the child's own intellectual understanding. We cannot just grasp and imitate anything; we cannot imitate things that are beyond our comprehension; we can only grasp and imitate things that are within our reach. Conversely, the things we can understand and imitate indicate our intellectual horizon. In Vygotsky's words:

> Let us explain this concept of the zone of proximal development and its meaning. Let us call, as this is becoming more and more generally accepted in contemporary pedology, the level of actual development which the child reached in the course of his or her development and which is established with the help of tasks solved by the child independently. Consequently, the level of actual development is the mental age in the usual sense in which it is used in pedology. We now in pedology refrain from calling exactly this the mental age, because, as we saw, it does not characterize mental development. The zone of proximal development of the child is the distance between the level of his actual development, established with the help of problems independently solved, and the level of the child's possible development, established with the help of problems solved by the child under the guidance of adults or in cooperation with his more intelligent partners. What is the level of actual development? When we from the viewpoint of the most naïve person ask what the level of actual development is – in simple words, what the problems that the child independently solves mean – the most usual answer will be that the level of the actual development of the child is determined by the functions that have already matured, the fruits of development. The child can independently do this, that, and that, thus the functions needed to independently do this, that, or that have matured. And the zone of proximal development, established with the help of problems which the child cannot solve independently, but can solve with help, what does that signify? The zone of proximal development refers to functions that have not yet matured, but are in the process of maturing, functions that mature tomorrow, that now are still in their embryonic form; functions that cannot be called the fruits of development, but the buds of development, the flowers of development, i.e. that which is only just maturing. The level of actual development characterizes the successes of development, the results of yesterday's development,

but the zone of proximal development characterizes tomorrow's mental development.

(Vygotsky in a talk delivered on 23 December 1933. See Vygotsky 1933/1935e, p. 42)

What Vygotsky was arguing here was that testing children twice, first without help and subsequently with help, gives us the lower and upper boundaries of the zone within which proper school instruction should move. The teacher should ideally present the child with problems that the child cannot yet fully solve independently, but is capable of solving with help. Such problems will be new and stimulating to the child and will propel the child's intellectual development forward. In order to solve these problems the child will have to use skills that are only just maturing. Of course, after enough practice even these new tasks and problems will become a matter of routine and will no longer be challenging to the child. The child has now realized its (former) zone of proximal development and it is time to move on and to offer new and more difficult tasks. These new tasks must lie within the child's next zone of proximal development. In this view, then, mental development constitutes a process of shifting boundaries: what once was a task within or even beyond the zone of proximal development has now become a task within the zone of actual development. What once could only be accomplished with help can now be accomplished independently. Viewed in this way, the concept of the zone of proximal development has three aspects that we must look at specifically. First, there is the dimension of time and the prognosis of mental development. Second, there is the dimension of the social-individual transition. Third, there is the idea that instruction is the leading factor in mental development (Valsiner and Van der Veer 1993).

As to the time dimension and the prognosis of mental development we can note the following. Vygotsky himself, and the researchers whom he referred to, were clearly interested in using mental tests as a prognostic device for individual children. Children were tested to get an idea about their future performance in school. The researchers found that their new method of dual testing (once without and once with help) was more indicative of the child's learning potential or intelligence than the standard procedure of just looking at the mental age or IQ scores. After all, children with the same IQ might have a different zone of proximal development as determined by the dual testing procedure. Thus, the new procedure allowed psychologists to make finer distinctions between children and to give better predictions of their future performance. Such information was viewed by the adherents of mental tests as vitally important for teachers at both primary and secondary school. In Chapter 6 we will see that this concept of repeated testing was partly rediscovered and partly reinvented in our time and led to a new trend in the mental testing tradition.

The second point to note is that the dual testing procedure involves the social-individual dimension. After all, what is claimed is that what the child can do now in cooperation, it will be able to do tomorrow independently. In other words, it is suggested that joint problem-solving actions precede and partially create individual problem-solving behavior. And we can now see clearly why the idea of the zone of proximal development must have appealed strongly to Vygotsky. After all, in Chapter 3 we have seen that for Vygotsky all higher mental functions originate in social interaction. He even stated a so-called sociogenetic law:

> In general we might say that the relations between higher mental functions once were genuine relations between people... Every function in the cultural development of the child appears twice, in two planes, first, the social, then the psychological, first between people as an interpsychological category, then within the child as an intrapsychological category.
>
> (Vygotsky 1931/1983, pp. 142–5)

This sociogenetic law essentially stated that higher mental processes and self-regulation originate in social interaction with a more able partner. What the child can do in cooperation now, it can do independently tomorrow. The stage of joint performance precedes that of autonomous performance. Now, the concept of the zone of proximal development seems a perfect illustration of that law. The test performance with help indicates the interpsychological stage of problem solving; the test performance without help the intrapsychological stage. What may have appealed to Vygotsky in the concept of the zone of proximal development was that it seemed a transposition of the idea of the sociogenetic law to the domain of prognosis. In that respect, the help and hints provided in a joint problem-solving situation are similar to the colored cards in the forbidden colors task (see Chapter 3). Both are essentially cultural tools provided by more able partners that the child utilizes to solve a problem. As the child grows older it will internalize these tools or shift to others in order to be able to solve the task independently. Because joint problem-solving precedes and partially creates individual problem solving (the sociogenetic law) the one can be used to predict the other (the concept of the zone of proximal development).

Finally, we should note that Vygotsky discussed the idea of the concept of proximal development in the context of education and, particularly, as a means to ensure good instruction. Ideally, instruction should be geared to the individual student, i.e. the instruction should fall into the zone of proximal development of the particular student. Instruction should not follow mental development (as determined by traditional tests) but create it. In Vygotsky's words:

> Only that instruction is good that runs ahead of development ... the correctly organized instruction of the child leads the child's mental development, calls into life a whole series of developmental processes that without instruction would have been altogether impossible.
> (Vygotsky 1933/1935a, pp. 15–16)

This was a view of the relationship between instruction and cognitive development that was not generally shared at the time. In the next sections we will come back to Vygotsky's more general view of the role of school instruction. However, before we do that it is useful to make a few concluding remarks about the function and historical fate of the concept of the zone of proximal development. As was mentioned above, Vygotsky introduced the concept in the context of the so-called leveling effect of schools. He wished to explain why bright pupils lost some of their edge in school. His ultimate explanation was quite simple: because the regular instruction in school does not create a (new) zone of proximal development for bright pupils, they will lose part of their edge.

> Why do the children with a high IQ tend to lose their high IQ during the four years of elementary school? The majority of the children who arrive with a high IQ ... are children who grew up in favorable circumstances ... One child grows up in a cultured family, where there are booklets, where they show him letters, where he is read to, but another child lives in a family where he never saw a printed letter. We test these children with the help of the Binet test and other ones, which are adapted to school knowledge, to the skills the children learned at school ... Is it surprising that the children who come from a more cultured family show a high IQ? We should be amazed about the opposite. Where do these children get their high IQ? They get it owing to the zone of proximal development, i.e. they run though their zone of proximal development earlier and therefore they end up with a relatively small zone of development, because to some extent they have already used it up.
> (Vygotsky 1933/1935e, pp. 51–2)

In essence, then, Vygotsky was arguing that children with a high IQ often – he even mentioned a percentage of 'more than seventy' (Vygotsky 1933/1935e, p. 51) – owe their high scores to the privileged environments in which they grew up. As soon as they enter school, they will spend a large part of the day in an environment where the circumstances are the same for everybody. Because the instruction is designed for the average child of that age the brighter children will be insufficiently challenged and will lose some of their mental superiority. That explanation is intriguing for different reasons.

First, it would seem that Vygotsky somewhat overestimated the influence of the school as a social equalizer. It is true that children from less privileged milieus will learn to read at school and in that sense will catch up with children who enter school already literate or semi-literate. But it is far from sure that they will *fully* catch up given that environmental differences in the form of the availability of books etc. will continue. Also, being environmentally privileged involves much more than being literate at a young age. It is possible that children from such milieus have also gained more knowledge and have learned more cognitive and meta-cognitive skills. Moreover, during their entire school period they will probably have more opportunities and facilities to increase their knowledge and improve their skills, and thus also gain more self-confidence. Thus, a strong leveling effect of school may not occur. In fact, both classic and modern researchers have posited the opposite effect, called the *Matthew effect*.[19] According to these researchers, for various reasons the small initial differences between children will be amplified rather than leveled during the school period. The idea is that early success or failure triggers a variety of consequences that increase the initially slight differences to form a wide gap. For example, initial success may lead to increased motivation, self-efficacy and effort, which in their turn may influence the child's future performance positively as well as lead to high expectations by the teachers, which in its turn might induce the teachers to give these pupils more challenging tasks and so on. Initial failure, on the contrary, might lead to a similar cascade of effects in the opposite direction. The net result would be a widening of initial differences. Unfortunately, although the arguments used in favor of both the leveling effect and the Matthew effect seem intuitively plausible, the fact is that after roughly 80 years of research we still don't seem to have much hard evidence for a general trend in either direction (Scarborough and Parker 2003). That is, we must leave open the possibility that it was in seeking an explanation for an artifact that Vygotsky elaborated the concept of the zone of proximal development.

Second, if we accept Vygotsky's viewpoint that most children with high IQs who enter school owe this high IQ to their privileged environment, then his whole plea for instruction in the zone of proximal development becomes potentially somewhat controversial. After all, in Vygotsky's reasoning, by offering stimulating instruction to bright children we create new horizons of mental development for them. Hence, the alleged leveling effect of schools would disappear and malicious critics might argue that Vygotsky's plea for instruction in the zone of proximal development essentially boiled down to advocating a practice that preserves cognitive differences between children that are based on social class. That would certainly have been a very unwelcome suggestion in the Soviet period.[20]

Historically, this is not what happened. The whole idea of repeatedly administering IQ tests during children's school careers met with opposition from the very beginning in all countries where it was suggested. Administering individual mental tests is time consuming and requires expertise, which is rather impractical in everyday school practice. For this reason the advocates of mental tests opted for compromises. One suggested solution was to form different *groups* of children according to their level of mental development (dull, average, bright) and to give them the instruction that corresponded with their average level. It was acknowledged, however, that putting children together who differed vastly in age but were intellectually on a par might have its limits (Odell 1922; 1930). However, other theorists opposed the idea of composing classrooms on the basis of mental test results altogether. They reasoned that the teacher's judgment was to be preferred, that test scores can be improved by training, that tests are unfair to certain groups, and so on. Historically, we may conclude that in most countries the massive attack by the testing movement on the educational system failed to a substantial degree: promotion is still largely based on chronological age; promotion and demotion are primarily based on the teacher's judgments; school achievements are still assessed on the basis of test questions designed by the teacher, and so on. The routine and frequent mental testing of school children never got a foothold and psychologists lost sight of the idea of dual testing as suggested by the concept of the zone of proximal development. When after decades of silence this idea resurfaced in the work of Feuerstein and in that of adherents of Vygotsky, researchers mostly focused on one of its aspects: some focused on the idea of dual testing as a prognostic device for the individual child; others focused on the idea of cooperation with more able partners as a source of mental development (see Chapter 6).

In fine, Vygotsky advanced the concept of the zone of proximal development in the context of the need for instruction to take account of the child's mental level.[21] The only fruitful instruction is that which stimulates the child, because it is just above the level of the child's independent performance. Vygotsky's explanation that the lack of such instruction causes the leveling effect of school may be doubted (as well as the effect itself), but strictly speaking this explanation is not relevant for an evaluation of the concept of the zone of proximal development itself. When the concept was rediscovered in the 1970s it caused a flurry of new and highly interesting empirical investigations and theoretical interpretations (cf. Chapter 6).

Education and Development

Previously, we stated that Vygotsky discussed the concept of the zone of proximal development in talks and writings that dealt with the relationship between education and mental development. We also saw that Vygotsky stated that instruction should run ahead of development, should call into life developmental processes. These statements raise the question of what exactly Vygotsky meant by the terms 'instruction' and 'development' and how he viewed their relationship. This was an issue that Vygotsky dealt with several times, notably in Chapter 6 of his *Thinking and Speech* (Vygotsky 1934a). In that chapter Vygotsky stated his own position while discussing three well-known views of the relationship between instruction and development.

According to the first view, ascribed to, among others, Piaget, instruction and development are mutually independent. Cognitive development rests upon maturational processes and has nothing to do with education. That is why Piaget in his efforts to study 'pure' cognitive development shied away from topics instructed in school: he was afraid to get ready-made answers based on school knowledge that had nothing to do with the child's own level of thinking. That is why he turned to topics where the child had no previous knowledge at all. This was also the reason that Piaget was interested in children's spontaneous concepts and not in the scientific concepts children use. The background assumption was that cognition and knowledge are independent things, that they are not related to each other. Cognition or intelligence is viewed as private property based on inheritance and maturation, which should be measured in its pure form, i.e. uncontaminated by instruction and other environmental factors. For education, this view implies that teachers can and must build on the effects of maturation, but that instruction itself cannot influence cognitive development in any fundamental way.

The second view, ascribed to James and Thorndike, stated that there can be no relationship between instruction and cognitive development, because they are essentially the same. Both instruction and development are based on the formation of associations; education and development are both based on a process of conditioning. At most one might say that the teacher creates the adequate conditions for successful conditioning to take place, but in this sense school has no fundamental advantage over life. Neither can we say that education calls into life intellectual processes that wouldn't have evolved otherwise. It is interesting to note that this view comes quite close to the view that Vygotsky himself defended in earlier years. In Chapter 2 we saw that in the early 1920s Vygotsky was quite impressed by Pavlov's theory of classical conditioning and that he couched learning in terms of conditioning. In that period he also saw the teacher's role in terms of facilitation; just like the gardener cannot force the plant to grow, the teacher cannot compel the pupil to learn. As we will see, in the 1930s Vygotsky considered this view to be one-sided. Of course, there is a lower boundary in instruction; we cannot just teach the child anything irrespective of his or her intellectual level. But beyond that lower boundary instruction is of fundamental importance for cognitive development.

The third view, which Vygotsky ascribed to Koffka, held that development is based on both maturation and instruction. According to Vygotsky, this view had several advantages. First, Koffka held that instruction and development are somehow related, although he did not specify exactly how. Second, Koffka formulated a new and promising view of instruction: instruction must create new structures or *Gestalts* of thinking. These structures are independent of content, which implies that once a child has mastered a certain structure it can apply that structure in other domains of knowledge as well. Thus, this view implies that instruction can lead to different types of results. Learning to type, for example, will teach the child just that and no more. It is hard to see how the child could profit from this skill in other areas. Learning to reason or learning specific heuristics, however, might yield much more. It is quite conceivable that such structures of thinking are applicable in other domains as well. Third, Koffka allowed for the possibility that instruction can go ahead of development, because mastering a new structure in one area may yield future results in other areas. In essence, then, Koffka defended a structural view of development (not unlike that of the later Piaget) in which education played a formative role.

It was Koffka's thinking about the relationship of instruction and development that most appealed to Vygotsky. He claimed that Koffka's theory was dualistic in that it posited an additive model for the influence of maturation and instruction without specifying their mutual relationship, but nevertheless it was Koffka's theory he took as a starting point for his own views and empirical investigations. Vygotsky's conclusion from these investigations[22] was that there are complex relationships between instruction and development. The major products of instruction in elementary school are *osoznanie* and *ovladenie*. *Osoznanie* can be translated as *becoming conscious of something* or *conscious realization* (French: *prise de conscience*). The child becomes capable of *reflecting* about his or her own actions and utterances. *Ovladenie* can be translated as *mastery* or *control*. Because the child consciously realizes what he or she is doing, he or she can *deliberately* carry out actions or operations. In other words, the child's actions are no longer at the mercy of environmental stimulation, because the child has mastered his or her own behavior. How did Vygotsky arrive at the concepts of *osoznanie* and *ovladenie*? Here Vygotsky's reasoning was rather general and based on examples. His favorite example was that of learning to write. What makes learning to write difficult for school children? In what sense is writing different from speaking? Vygotsky asserted that writing is difficult, because it is maximally different from inner speech (see Chapter 3). Because inner speech is addressed to oneself it can be maximally abbreviated, condensed and predicative. That is, one may leave out verbs, names, specifications and so on, because the speaker and listener coincide and all these details are known beforehand. In oral speech one must be more specific because the listener doesn't share all the information. Finally, in writing, or written speech as Vygotsky called it, one must be still more specific, because the recipient is not present in the same physical environment. For example, one cannot write 'When I stood here he insulted me', because the words 'here' and 'he' have no specified meaning outside the context. Thus, in writing one must spell out all sorts of details that are not necessary in normal conversation, let alone in inner speech. In order to do so the child must think carefully about what message he or she wants to express and what exact information the recipient needs to understand the message. Of course, in learning to write the children must also learn that sounds can be conveyed by symbols, that words consist of syllables, and so on. In that process, they become more conscious of the structure of their own language. Finally, writing is different from speaking in that it requires a different motive. Oral speech takes place mostly in conversations where the things one says are a reply to what the other person says. Oral speech is, in other words, largely stimulus driven, largely motivated by the other person's utterances. Writing, however, for example writing a letter, requires a conscious decision, a special motivation not called forth by an immediately preceding reply.

In sum, there are many differences between speaking and writing which make it understandable that writing is difficult for young children. Writing is a skill that requires conscious control or deliberate mastery. At the same time, when learning to write, children become much more aware of the properties of their own language; they realize that it has a certain structure.

Now, Vygotsky posited that what takes place in becoming literate is a more general phenomenon in school. Children learn to deliberately master certain skills and thereby become more aware of the processes they previously carried out involuntarily. Learning to write feeds back on one's understanding of oral speech; learning grammar makes one aware of certain structural properties of one's native tongue; learning a foreign language makes one aware of the peculiarities of one's own language; learning mathematics yields a deeper understanding of arithmetic, and so on. Things that children previously did spontaneously and without much understanding now become fully understood and under conscious control. Hence Vygotsky's claim that the main products of school instruction are reflection (*osoznanie*) and mastery (*ovladenie*). Moreover, as said before, the understanding of one topic has feedback effects on the understanding of other topics. This led Vygotsky to state that the old doctrine of the formal discipline[23] had some truth to it after all and that instruction can have structural effects on cognition that go beyond the topic and knowledge taught. Thus instruction creates things that were definitely not there in the first place. Instruction and cognitive development must be distinguished and instruction calls into life structural changes in cognition that wouldn't have taken place otherwise. With this position Vygotsky emphasized the leading role of school instruction and specified (with the concepts of reflection and mastery or control) a mechanism for its restructuring effects. He claimed that this position was confirmed by empirical investigations. However, the only investigation that has been preserved in any detail was that into the interplay of everyday and scientific concepts, carried out by Vygotsky's doctoral student Shif. It is to this study that we now turn.

The Role of Scientific Concepts

When children enter school they already know many everyday concepts, that is, concepts acquired outside of the context of explicit school instruction. Characteristic of these concepts is that they have not been introduced to the child in a systematic and interconnected fashion. Children mostly do not know how different concepts hang together and it is not guaranteed that the concepts adequately cover all the essential aspects of a certain area of knowledge. For scientific concepts this is different. Ideally, the teacher teaches them as an interconnected whole and it may be assumed that the concepts reflect the latest scientific insights in that domain of knowledge (to the extent that this is possible and feasible). In accordance with his general view of the relationship between instruction and development, Vygotsky believed that scientific concepts build on but also restructure the child's everyday concepts. Shif's (1935) investigation was an attempt to test this hypothesis. At the same time, however, the investigation was an attempt to refute certain findings and interpretations put forth by Piaget, which explains part of the setup and methodology. As seen above, Piaget had claimed that one should study children's spontaneous concepts, because in his view only these reflect their genuine thinking. In one of his investigations, Piaget (1924) investigated the child's understanding of the words 'although' and 'because' by presenting them sentences that ended with these words and asking the children to complete them. Thus, he presented such sentences as

'The pilot crashed his airplane, because . . .' and 'The boy was naughty, although . . .'. Shif decided to copy this procedure but to test both younger and older children and to test their understanding of these words in both everyday and scientific contexts. With Vygotsky she believed that the systematic introduction of such words as 'because' and 'although' in a scientific context might influence the child's understanding of these words in an everyday context as well. In order to test that hypothesis, she interviewed children from both the second and fourth grade of elementary school, presenting them sentences about both everyday and scientific topics. The scientific topics were taken from a subject that the children were taught at school, namely civics (*obshchestvovedenie*), which at that time was equivalent to an explanation of the Soviet worldview. Thus, she presented children with such test sentences as 'The capitalists prepare for a war against the USSR, because. . .' and 'There are still workers who believe in god, although . . .' Now what did Shif find? We will focus on her results concerning the completion of sentences ending with 'because'.

In the second grade, children could correctly finish 59 per cent of the 'because' sentences about everyday topics and 80 per cent of those about the scientific subject matter. However, when questioned about their answers in the scientific domain, the children showed a rather stereotypical understanding: the children could explain their answers, but their explanations seemed to repeat the explanations taught at school in a rather schematic fashion. This was not the case for the everyday topics, but here Shif found that the children frequently gave tautological answers (e.g. 'The pilot crashed his airplane, because he crashed his airplane') or had difficulty explaining their answers. In her view, these results meant that at this age everyday and scientific answers have both their strong and weak points. In the scientific domain, children provided more adequate answers and could more often advance an explanation. However, their answers were rather stereotyped. In the domain of everyday life, the answers were less stereotyped but the number of correct answers was lower and the children had more trouble explaining their answers.

In the fourth grade, the picture was different. Now Shif found 81 per cent of correct answers in the everyday domain and 82 per cent of correct answers in the scientific domain for the 'because' sentences.

Moreover, Shif found that now the scientific answers had lost their schematic nature, the children now seemed to fully understand the subject matter and no longer simply repeated learned answers verbatim. How to explain this set of results? The explanation that Shif provided was as follows. Apparently, in school instruction the children are introduced to causal thinking, which implies the frequent use of 'because' constructions. Although the children do not fully understand this way of thinking, they become apt at using causal arguments and explaining them. In everyday life, however, this type of reasoning and explanation still lags behind (hence the lower number of correct answers for everyday 'because' sentences at this age). However, with a few years of instruction the picture changes dramatically. They not only become children capable of fully understanding causal arguments in scientific thought, but this manner of thinking also spreads to everyday life. Children can now reason causally about everyday events. The children have learned to use the 'because' construction in a deliberate and conscious fashion. Ideally, the child's concepts and his or her manner of reasoning now combine the strong aspects of everyday and scientific reasoning, i.e. the child's answers will be concrete and fully understood and yet based on scientific arguments. Such a view implies that instruction has created a zone of proximal development by introducing the child to scientific causal reasoning which, once mastered, spreads to other domains of the child's thinking. At the same time, scientific understanding is only complete when it is enriched with the concrete experiential knowledge of daily life. To give an example: the child's everyday concept of a farmer may be that of a person in exotic clothes who is breeding cattle and growing corn. The scientific concept may emphasize that the farmer is an entrepreneur operating in a market economy. But a full-fledged understanding of what a farmer is requires elements from both domains of knowledge; both experiential richness and scientific rigor. This is why Vygotsky talked about everyday and scientific concepts in terms of mutual enrichment.

Shif's investigation into the use of scientific concepts was one of the many investigations that Vygotsky supervised in this period. Both its conclusions and its methodology can be criticized on various grounds (Van der Veer and Valsiner 1991). But to Vygotsky this and the other investigations pointed to one fundamental conclusion:

instruction does fundamentally influence cognitive development and it does so by introducing the children to a scientific way of thinking. In mastering this way of thinking the children become capable of the conscious and deliberate use of certain skills and certain forms of reasoning. Things the children previously carried out automatically and without thinking now potentially fall under the reign of reflection. School, by introducing children to scientific thought, has a fundamental restructuring influence on intellectual development. Education leads children to levels of thinking they wouldn't have reached otherwise.

Conclusions

In the final years of his life Vygotsky once again dealt with the issue of education and development. In his lectures at the Moscow State Pedagogical Institute and the Herzen Pedagogical Institute in Leningrad he could hardly ignore that issue. Vast numbers of children from widely differing socio-economic and ethnic backgrounds entered the Soviet school and both psychologists, educationalists and pedologists were actively involved in trying to solve the problems that this massive invasion created. Renowned scientists all over the world suggested that mental tests might be used to improve the fairness and efficiency of the educational system and it is obvious that Vygotsky followed the international discussion about the use of mental tests in schools very attentively. It was in this context that he came across the idea of the zone of proximal development. This idea fitted perfectly well with the general orientation of the theory of the higher cultural functions which he had been elaborating in previous years. That theory stated that seemingly private intellectual abilities originate in social interactions with adults or more able peers. In these social interactions children learn to master specific cultural tools that enable them to solve intellectual problems and master their own behavior. Instruction at school is a special and privileged form of social interaction. Teachers introduce children to the scientific way of thinking by teaching them coherent systems of scientific concepts in specific areas. These scientific concepts are dependent upon the children's everyday concepts but will also restructure and enrich them. The rational scientific approach will spread to the child's everyday thinking and will allow the child to carry out his or her actions in a conscious and deliberate manner. This means that school instruction creates something over and above normal social interaction. Formal instruction is necessary to lift the child to the level of systemic scientific thinking. Instruction in the zone of proximal development creates new levels of cognitive development that would not have been reached otherwise.

Vygotsky's views on the relationship between education and development as explained above are quite complex and trigger a great number of questions and it is only natural that contemporary researchers have accepted or elaborated different aspects of them. For example, some researchers have revived the idea of repeated mental testing as a prognostic device. Possible questions that can come up in this research area are, for example, what form should a standardized dual testing procedure take? And does the dual testing procedure indeed yield better prognostic information than the classic procedure? Other researchers have concentrated upon the idea that social interaction or cooperation precedes and partially creates individual abilities. For example, one may investigate whether the working together of pupils of different abilities is advantageous for the less bright pupils. Or, one may wish to compare classic frontal instruction with forms where the pupils jointly solve problems. Still other researchers have focused on the idea that formal instruction as such creates unique abilities. This might lead one to compare the cognitive abilities of literate with those of illiterate children or to compare the cognitive abilities of children who attended a western-type school with those of children who went to a non-western school or did not attend school at all. In sum, there is an enormous variety of questions that one can ask starting from Vygotsky's account of the relationship between education and development. Not all of these questions will be equally fruitful and not all of Vygotsky's claims will survive modern criticism. But it is obvious that approximately 75 years after their first publication Vygotsky's educational writings still manage to inspire a great number of researchers and stimulate many interesting empirical investigations. In Chapter 6 we shall discuss the major trends in this area of research.

Chapter 5

Cross-cultural Education

Introduction

In the preceding chapters we have seen that Vygotsky argued that higher intellectual abilities rest upon the acquisition of cultural tools. The most fundamental of these cultural tools (e.g. literacy, scientific concepts) are transmitted in school instruction. This view implied that there are major intellectual differences between children who did or did not receive formal school instruction and between children from different cultural or ethnic backgrounds. Should one find major intellectual differences between children or adults from various ethnic backgrounds, then these should be attributed to the different educational systems and not to differences in innate ability (see Chapter 3). Vygotsky's view may be seen as plausible, but it was by no means the only view and it still lacked an empirical foundation. It was for this reason that Vygotsky and Luria pondered the possibility of doing an empirical investigation of the cognitive abilities of persons in an area where the educational system was in transition. In the late 1920s and early 1930s there was no shortage of such areas, because the Soviet Union was gradually introducing formal western-type school instruction in all of its republics. The idea was to 'lift' the level of education to western standards and also, of course, to get rid of all sorts of local ideas and customs (e.g. religions) that the Soviet regime considered obsolete or dangerous. The idea was to create the new Soviet man, who regarded the local cultural customs with contempt and was loyal to the communist worldview. Indeed, the very idea of 'culture' or 'cultural variation' became associated with ideas of nationalism, which the Soviet state wanted to avoid at all costs (Ageyev 2003).

The empirical investigation that Vygotsky and Luria planned to carry out was not the first one of this type (Kurek 2004). Psychologists and medical anthropologists had investigated the intellectual abilities and physical properties (e.g. size of cranium) of representatives of various minorities in Central Asia such as the Chuvash (cf. Efimov 1931), the Oyrot (Zaporozhets 1930), the Tungus (Bulanov 1930), and the Uzbeks (Shishov 1928; Shtilerman 1928; Solov'ev 1929). Using mental tests such as the Binet-Simon test or the test developed by Rossolimo, they invariably found that the average IQ scores of members of the ethnic minorities were very low compared to those of native Russians (cf. Kurek 2004, p. 42). Many of these investigations were published in the journal *Pedologiya*, where Vygotsky was on the editorial board, and Zaporozhets was one of Vygotsky's students at the time. Thus, Vygotsky and Luria were well aware of the existing cross-cultural investigations into cognitive abilities and their results. In fact, as Kurek (2004) has shown, Vygotsky's (1929b) own paper in *Pedologiya* on the best way to investigate the cognitive abilities of ethnic minorities can partially be seen as a comment on Shtilerman's (1928) earlier article. In his paper, and without mentioning Shtilerman's name,[24] Vygotsky argued that it is not enough to adjust one or more items of western IQ tests to the local culture (as Shtilerman had done), but that one should thoroughly investigate the whole local culture with the cultural tools it provides, because this culture creates specific cognitive abilities. With this goal in mind, he pleaded for the regular undertaking of pedological field studies in the remote areas of the Soviet Union (Vygotsky 1929b). It would take several years, however, before Vygotsky and Luria managed to carry out this idea in practice (Van der Veer and Valsiner 1991).

Cognitive Abilities in Central Asia

To test their hypothesis that higher psychological processes are different in different cultures and that they change under the influence of cultural changes (notably changes in the schooling system), Vygotsky and Luria turned to Uzbekistan. In the summers of 1931 and 1932, Luria traveled to the Fergana valley and together with some

10 to 15 collaborators, students and interpreters investigated the way of thinking of the local inhabitants of several villages (Van der Veer and Valsiner 1991). Unlike previous investigators, they did not satisfy themselves with administering the usual IQ tests, but made use of a whole variety of tasks and tests to tap the intellectual abilities of their subjects. Thus, they investigated the subjects' susceptibility to visual illusions, their classification of colors and geometrical figures, their use of abstract names for groups of objects, the ability to make use of syllogisms, problem solving, imagination, religious thinking, self-awareness, and so on (Luria 1974; 1976). To do this under laboratory conditions would have been relatively easy, although time consuming, but in the setting of the Uzbek culture it proved a most laborious task. Luria and his co-workers first had to establish friendly relations with the inhabitants of the villages so that the test questions would seem natural, unaggressive and polite. Much care was taken to develop problems and questions that would seem meaningful to the participants; many problems were presented in the familiar format of 'riddles' and discussed in friendly group conversations; recording of the answers was done in an unobtrusive way; and the prepared tasks were only introduced when the atmosphere seemed right. Obviously, all conversations were conducted in Uzbek and female Islamic subjects had to be interviewed at home by female experimenters. In sum, the two lengthy visits to Uzbekistan had all the features of an anthropological field expedition and many cups of tea were consumed before the data-gathering process could commence (Luria 1976, pp. 16–17).

In the eyes of Vygotsky and Luria, Uzbekistan was quite suited for the kind of investigation they had in mind, because several potentially relevant circumstances were in transition. Thus, the Soviets had organized regular schools and evening courses and it was possible to investigate subjects who had attended them and to compare them with those who had not. Also, the Soviet authorities were busy eradicating private agriculture, forcing the private farmers (*kulak*) to become part of the huge collective farms (*kolkhoz*),[25] which made it possible to investigate the mentality of those who formed part of the *kolkhoz* with those who did not. In sum, it seemed possible to investigate both the influence of larger societal changes and the influence of school instruction on the cognitive processes of the Uzbek subjects.

In order to investigate the subjects' cognitive performance, Luria typically divided them into five groups of different 'educational level' or 'degree of primitivism'. The first group consisted of illiterate women from remote villages who hardly left their houses. The second group consisted of private farmers from the same remote villages. The third group consisted of women who attended short-term courses, but had enjoyed no or hardly any previous formal education. The fourth group was made up of active *kolkhoz* workers in collectivized villages. Finally, the fifth group consisted of women students admitted to a teacher training college. Luria nowhere provided any criteria for his ranking of subjects according to their degree of 'primitivism', but it is nevertheless more or less clear what he had in mind. The term 'primitivism' was in no way tied to supposed innate abilities, but referred to a limited repertoire of cultural tools (see Chapter 3). Thus, subjects who could not read or write, or could not use scientific concepts, would be regarded 'primitive' or 'backward' (cf. Van der Veer and Valsiner 1991). With hindsight, we can see that those subjects who had the least contact with the world at large, with the products of the larger (western) culture, were deemed most primitive or backward by Vygotsky and Luria. That is, they interpreted cultural differences in developmental terms and considered literacy and rational, abstract, scientific thinking as the highest achievements of human thinking. The crucial question was whether access to schooling and new cultural tools would indeed be reflected in measurable different patterns of thinking (see Van der Veer and Valsiner 1991, pp. 251–3, for several methodological problems with this type of research).

Classification

One of the tasks used by Luria and his colleagues was that of the grouping or classification of similar objects. Subjects were presented with the drawing of four objects and had to decide which three objects belonged together. This was a well-known task in psychology and, in fact, Petrova (1925) had used this and other tasks used by Luria in her research with children (see Chapter 3). Just like Petrova, Luria found that some subjects preferred to join objects in one group that are frequently seen together in some concrete everyday context. For example, Luria (1976, p. 57) showed a subject drawings of a glass, a saucepan, a pair of spectacles, and a bottle. The conversation went as follows:

SUBJECT: 'These three go together, but why you've put the spectacles here, I don't know. Then again, they also fit in. If a person doesn't see too well, he has to put them on to eat dinner.'

EXPERIMENTER: 'But one fellow told me one of these things didn't belong to this group.'

SUBJECT: 'Probably that kind of thinking runs in his blood. But I say they all belong here. You can't cook in the glass, you have to fill it. For cooking, you need the saucepan, and to see better, you need the spectacles. We need all four of these things, that's why they were put here.'

Another subject replied as follows (after Luria 1976, pp. 57–8):

SUBJECT: 'I don't know which of the things doesn't fit here. Maybe it's the bottle? You can drink tea out of a glass – that's useful. The spectacles are also useful. But there's vodka in the bottle – that's bad.'

EXPERIMENTER: 'Could you say that the spectacles don't belong to this group?'

SUBJECT: 'No, spectacles are also a useful thing.'
[The experimenter explains that three objects can be termed cooking vessels.]

EXPERIMENTER: 'So would it be right to say that the spectacles don't fit in this group?'

SUBJECT: 'No, I think the bottle doesn't belong here. It's harmful!'

EXPERIMENTER: 'But you can use one word – vessels – for these three, right?'

SUBJECT: 'If you're cooking something on the fire, you've got to use the eye-glasses or you just won't be able to cook.'

Other subjects gave similar answers, i.e. where Luria expected them to classify the objects according to some abstract property (e.g. that they are made of glass, or that they are cooking vessels), the subjects preferred to look at their concrete usage in some practical context. Luria concluded that the subjects:

> either disregard generic terms or considered them irrelevant, in no way essential to the business of classification. Clearly, different psychological processes determined their manner of grouping which hinged on concrete, situational thinking rather than on abstract operations which entail the generalizing function of language.
> (Luria 1976, p. 77)

Luria's finding replicated Petrova's (1925) findings, who also found that some children focus on concrete properties or functional usage rather than on abstract properties (see Chapter 3). What was new in Luria's investigations was that he managed to link this tendency to the degree of schooling the subjects had enjoyed: unlike their illiterate compatriots, Uzbek subjects who had enjoyed one or two years of schooling did employ abstract or categorical classification criteria (Luria 1976, p. 78).

Reasoning

Luria and his co-workers also presented the Uzbek subjects with problems of the following form: it takes three hours to go from A to B, and two hours to go from B to C; how long does it take to go from A to C? Here again, as the investigators used the names of existing villages in the vicinity instead of using letters, the subjects without any schooling tended to rely on their own experience. That is, rather than drawing a logical conclusion from the hypothetical information presented in the premises, they reverted to concrete memories or practical considerations about the conditions of the road, the possibility of fatigue, and so on. Moreover, they experienced particular difficulties with premises that flatly contradicted their own everyday experience. The following example is illustrative (after Luria 1976, p. 131):

EXPERIMENTER: 'Suppose it were to take six hours to get from here to Fergana on foot, and a bicycle was twice as slow?'
SUBJECT: 'Then a bicycle would get there in three hours!'
EXPERIMENTER: 'No, a teacher gave this problem as an exercise – suppose the bicycle were twice as slow.'
SUBJECT: 'If the cyclist makes good time, he will get to Fergana in two and a half or three hours. According to your problem, though, if the bicycle breaks down on the way, he'll arrive later, of course. If there's a breakdown, he'll be two or three hours late.'
[The experimenter repeats the problem.]
SUBJECT: 'Probably he'll get there in eight hours . . . probably, if the bicycle breaks down, he'll be two hours late . . .'
EXPERIMENTER: 'And if the bicycle doesn't break down, but that's simply the way the problem says it is?'
SUBJECT: 'If it doesn't break down, he'll make it not just in six hours but in three.'

Luria (1976, p. 132) concluded that such answers revealed a tendency to operate on a concrete practical level rather than on a hypothetical one. In his view, the formal operation of problem solving presents major, sometimes insurmountable, difficulties for the Uzbek subjects with no schooling. As soon as they had enjoyed one or two years of schooling, however, the subjects no longer had any difficulties with hypothetical problems. According to Luria (1976, p. 133), 'the significance of schooling lies not just in the acquisition of new knowledge, but in the creation of new motives and formal modes of discursive verbal and logical thinking divorced from immediate practical experience'.

Conclusions

The results of the investigations in Uzbekistan confirmed Vygotsky's and Luria's expectations: apparently, there are major differences between the ways of thinking of subjects from different cultural backgrounds. Cultures provide their members with sets of cultural tools that determine their modes of thought. There is no doubt that Vygotsky and Luria interpreted these results in developmental terms. Concrete, situational thinking was seen as an inferior type of intellectual operation characteristic of subjects who had not enjoyed formal instruction in school. As soon as subjects received one or two years of instruction in a western-type school, they became capable of abstract, rational, scientific thinking. In the eyes of Vygotsky and Luria, the access to (western) culture allowed the Uzbek population to make 'a leap of centuries' (Luria 1976, p. 164).

The results found by Luria and his colleagues have been confirmed repeatedly in various parts of the world. As soon as one leaves the western world, subjects will tend to solve the problems posed by psychologists in the manner presented above. That is, subjects will be unwilling to reason from hypothetical premises, will interpret problems in a practical, situational manner, and so on. We also find that the willingness to reason abstractly, disregarding the genuine circumstances, is present in subjects who have attended several years of (western) schooling. But we nowadays pose questions that go further. Which aspects of schooling are instrumental in changing the subjects' way of thinking? Does all formal instruction have the same repercussions or were the results that Luria found tied to a specific type of training in a specific type of school? Is it literacy or the acquisition of a scientific mode of reasoning that causes the cognitive changes? Or does it depend on the type of literacy? And are we allowed to interpret such cognitive changes in developmental terms? These questions are important and in Chapter 6 we shall try to answer several of them. But even if the answers to such questions would prove that Vygotsky's and Luria's conclusions were wanting, it remains important to state once more that from a historical point of view their views were most innovative. Unlike many of their contemporaries, they rejected innate, genetic differences as an explanation for differences in thinking between various ethnic groups. Indeed, the message of the cultural-historical theory of the higher psychological processes was that higher modes of thought are 'products of social history – they are subject to change when the basic forms of social practice are altered' (Luria 1976, p. 164).

In Chapter 1 we already indicated that the results of the investigations in Uzbekistan did not meet with official approval. After the first preliminary reports arrived in Moscow, the authorities decided to investigate the entire investigation in great detail. As said before, any investigation of local minorities had become somewhat explosive because of the fear of 'nationalism'. But the authorities were also troubled by the fact that participants in the *kolkhoz*, real communists perhaps, had been pictured by Luria as limited concrete thinkers. Razmyslov, the head of the commission appointed to investigate Luria's Uzbek research project, gave the following damaging example in his final report (after Razmyslov 1934/2000, p. 52):

EXPERIMENTER: 'A rich landowner got the idea to cultivate cattle and the cattle began to appear like flies.'
SUBJECT: 'How is that possible that the cattle were like flies? He is a rich landowner, so his cattle are always as big as elephants.'
EXPERIMENTER: 'Assume that his cattle became like flies.'
SUBJECT: 'We are moving toward socialism. The Soviet authorities took from the landowner all of his possessions and all of his cattle and did not leave even a fly, i.e. cattle that were no bigger than a fly. The landowner's cattle cannot grow thin; if he only had cattle like flies, that would mean that the landowner had been dispossessed.'
[The experimenter concludes that it was impossible to persuade the subject.]

Razmyslov observed that Luria on the basis of this protocol concluded that the subject was a concrete situational thinker, incapable of abstract thought, and operating at a lower intellectual level. Meanwhile, what Razmyslov (ibid., p. 52) read in this protocol was 'sound thinking demonstrating a highly developed political consciousness'. In other words, Luria had characterized members of the Uzbek minority who honestly and wholeheartedly participated in the building of socialism as limited concrete thinkers who still had to make a leap of centuries. Apart from all other considerations, that was politically a very unwise thing to do, of course. In the explosive mix of political terror, suppressed nationalism and Russian chauvinism, the Party couldn't use criticisms of active *kolkhoz* members. The immediate result of Razmyslov's report was that all data of the investigations in Uzbekistan disappeared in Luria's private files only to reappear again in the 1970s. And even then, after 40 years had passed, he could not publish all of his findings, nor had his conclusions lost all their pungency. Take his words in the preface of his book: 'Only the radical restructuring of the economy, the rapid elimination of illiteracy, and the removal of the Moslem influence could achieve, over and above an expansion in world view, a genuine revolution in cognitive activity' (Luria 1976, p. vi). That certainly is a conclusion that even nowadays might lead to lengthy and heated political debates.

Notes

1. Stanislavsky worked with Tolstoy and Chekhov and developed the famous 'method acting' which, among other things, demanded that actors pay close attention to important unspoken messages within the text. In the final chapter of his last work *Thinking and Speech* (1934a) Vygotsky returned to Stanislavsky's work to illustrate the importance of understanding motivation for our understanding of other persons' words.
2. Vygotsky followed Aikhenvald's (1872–1928) courses at Shanyavsky University and apparently knew Aikhenvald personally. In 1920, when a severe attack of tuberculosis threatened to kill him, it was Aikhenvald whom Vygotsky asked to take care of the posthumous publications of his writings. A few years later Aikhenvald was forced to emigrate to Berlin where he lived in one house with the formalist Viktor Shklovsky (1893–1984) and became good friends with the novelist Vladimir Nabokov (1899–1977) (Chamberlain 2006).
3. Characteristic of this stage of Vygotsky's thinking is that he recorded breathing patterns of persons who read Bunin's story by means of a pneumograph and claimed that their breathing was light or gentle. Thus by narrating the story in a non-chronological order Bunin created a lightness of style and a corresponding breathing pattern that contrasted with the sad content of the story. We here witness the tremendous change in Vygotsky's approach:

it is no longer the reader who creates his own subjective story on the basis of a framework supplied by the writer but the writer who by means of specific techniques elicits certain effects in the body and mind of the reader.
4. While Pavlov always spoke of reflexes, in *Educational Psychology* Vygotsky uses both 'reflexes' and 'reactions'. In later years, he would entirely switch to 'reactions', the importance being in his view that the term 'reflexes' is used for purely physiological processes, whereas the term 'reactions' denotes both the physiological and the mental part of the response. The head of his department, Kornilov, greatly favored the term 'reactions' (cf. Van der Veer 2007).
5. Or, AM = IR + CR, where AM is Animal Mind, IR is Innate Reflexes, CR is Conditional Reflexes. The conditional reflexes themselves are the product of IR and IP, where IP is Individual Experience. Hence Vygotsky's formula for the animal mind M = IR + (IR times IP).
6. Or, HM = IR + CR + HE + SE + DE, where HM is Human Mind, HE is Historical Experience, SE is Social Experience, and DE is Doubled Experience.
7. It is interesting that at this stage – unlike James (1920), for example – Vygotsky was rather dismissive about testing and grading individual students. His arguments were that the testing situation is by necessity rather contrived and that the idea of general intelligence or giftedness is a fiction (cf. Vygotsky 1930/1997, p. 237).
8. One may of course encourage children to actively search for necessary information in books or on the internet but although this is fun and although it is possible that the information thus found is retained better it is surely not the quickest way to obtain new knowledge, nor is the quality of the information guaranteed. A coherent lecture about some topic would still seem to be an indispensable means of transmitting what Vygotsky called social and historical experience.
9. Experts now generally hold that sign languages are, in linguistic terms, as rich and complex as any oral language (and that signed languages contain plenty of abstract terms) and that there is no reason to suppose that deaf-mute children cannot reach an adequate intellectual level.

10. In the case of feeble-minded children, primitiveness would be a secondary symptom to be distinguished from the primary symptoms that are caused by some organic defect.
11. Nowadays these issues are still hotly debated. Research has shown that many species produce and use tools to obtain food and that different groups of animals belonging to the same species may have different customs and in that sense culture (cf. De Waal 2001). Also, several researchers have claimed that different species show the rudiments of language. As a result, those defending the unique nature of humans have felt it necessary to shift criteria (e.g. by claiming that animals don't use tools to *make* tools or that animals cannot produce *complex* sentences).
12. Here he was debatably interpreting anthropological findings from non-western cultures as if they represented earlier stages in human history.
13. A similar view was more recently voiced by Sacks (1989, p. 41): 'It is clear that thought and language have quite separate (biological) origins, that the world is examined and mapped and responded to long before the advent of language, that there is a huge range of thinking – in animals, or infants – long before the emergence of language . . . it is obvious to every parent, or pet lover . . . A human being is not mindless or mentally deficient without language, but he is severely restricted in the range of his thoughts, confined, in effect, to an immediate, small world.'
14. Elsewhere Vygotsky claimed that biological evolution and historical development (say, the last 50,000 to 100,000 years) overlapped in time, but speculated that biological evolution is much too slow to have any relevant effects within the time frame of historical development. What changed enormously over this period was human culture, of course. The vast differences between Neanderthal man or Cro Magnon man and present-day human beings are, therefore, entirely due to the effects of culture, notably language and technology. This view implied that if a time machine would bring a Cro Magnon baby to our modern world, the baby's mental development would be indistinguishable from ours (cf. Barash 1986).

15. The neurologist Sacks, who is influenced by the writings of Vygotsky's collaborator Aleksandr Luria, likewise contends that 'language can grossly alter cerebral development' (Sacks 1989, p. 110).
16. This view is shared by Sacks (1995, pp. xvii-xviii), who believes we need 'a new view of the brain, a sense of it not as programmed and static, but rather as dynamic and active, a supremely efficient adaptive system geared for evolution and change, ceaselessly adapting to the needs of the organism . . . This sense of the brain's remarkable plasticity, its capacity for the most striking adaptations . . . has come to dominate my own perception of my patients and their lives'.
17. Both the finding itself and Vygotsky's explanation (see further) can be doubted. Should the finding be real, then a simple statistical explanation (regression toward the mean with repeated testing) must be ruled out first.
18. Vygotsky's (1933/1935e) statements about the relative success of bright children as compared to average and dull children seem to have been borrowed from Torgerson (1926).
19. The name of the effect is derived from the parable of the talents in the gospel of St Matthew (25: 29): 'For unto every one that hath shall be given, and he shall have abundance: but from him that hath not shall be taken away even that which he hath.' The term 'Matthew effect' was introduced by Merton (1968) and became popular in education through Walberg and Tsai (1983) and Stanovich (1986). However, the (possible) effect itself and the reference to the biblical passage were already known and discussed in the 1910s and 1920s by such researchers as Starch and Henmon (e.g. Henmon 1920; Reed 1924).
20. Of course, in various countries, there have been educationalists and politicians who wish the school to have a leveling effect and who have tried to use the school to undo what they see as unjust initial differences in opportunity.
21. We know of one publication where Vygotsky suggests that pretend play can be a source of the zone of proximal development. In playing the roles of adults, the child as it were rises above his own mental level ('is a head taller than himself' (Vygotsky 1933/1966)).

Theoretically, this suggestion was not elaborated upon. We may think of the child's pretend play in terms of deferred imitation and argue with Vygotsky that children can only imitate what they can almost understand. But the differences to the concept of the zone of development in instruction are substantial: in play the child actively selects the roles it wants to play and no help or hints as to the proper performance are provided. Thinking about play may give us a key to understanding informal learning, an area which received little emphasis in Vygotsky's work.

22. Although Vygotsky mentions that several empirical investigations were carried out under his guidance, these were not discussed in any detail. The results of the investigations were described in unpublished master's theses which may have been lost.

23. The idea was that the teaching of certain formal disciplines (e.g. Latin, mathematics) would instill certain skills in pupils that they can profitably use in mastering other topics, e.g. learning mathematics would yield analytic abilities that would make one more proficient in other areas as well (*learning transfer*). In Vygotsky's time this was a hotly debated topic and it still is. See, for example, the work of Scribner and Cole (1981), and Lave (1988).

24. Kurek (2004, pp. 241–5) interprets this silence negatively, arguing that Vygotsky did not want to mention Shtilerman's name, because he wished to present several of Shtilerman's ideas as his own. This is not the place to discuss that accusation, but it seems to me entirely unfounded. A more sympathetic interpretation would be that Vygotsky preferred to criticize the approach rather than the person.

25. The whole operation resulted in massive famine and death (according to eyewitness accounts the corpses were lying in the streets). Conquest (1986) has estimated that approximately 14 million people died as a result of the collectivization and dekulakization (cf. Medvedev 1974; Van der Veer and Valsiner 1991).

Part 3

The Reception, Influence and Relevance of Vygotsky's Work Today

Chapter 6

Contemporary Educational Research

Introduction

In the preceding chapters we reviewed a number of Vygotsky's ideas that are directly or indirectly relevant for education. Many of these ideas were still insufficiently elaborated upon when Vygotsky died at the age of 37. His Russian collaborators and students tried to work out his ideas in various directions despite active obstruction by the authorities. After the Pedology Decree of 1936 it was difficult to get access to Vygotsky's books and writings and references to his work in the scientific literature were discouraged. A number of Vygotsky's co-workers and students, however, were able to continue his line of research on a small scale and when the ban on his work was gradually lifted it turned out that they were able to seize major positions in the Soviet academic system. Such former colleagues as Luria, Leontiev, El'konin and Zaporozhets slowly and cautiously began promoting Vygotsky's work and negotiating for the republication of his writings in Russian and English. This eventually resulted in various Russian editions of Vygotsky's collected writings (Vygotsky 1956; 1960; 1982a; 1982b; 1983a; 1983b; 1984a; 1984b) and in the first publications of Vygotsky's books in English (Vygotsky 1962; 1965) and other languages. As a result, different waves of Vygotskian-inspired investigations emerged in different countries in different periods. Moreover, the researchers in different countries were not always well aware of each other's research due to political and linguistic barriers. Russian elaborations of Vygotsky's seminal ideas, for example, are still relatively little known in Europe and the United States, because of the Soviet tradition to publish primarily in Russian scientific journals. Russian researchers, in their turn, had difficulties in getting access to international scientific journals and books and at times were insufficiently aware of what Vygotskian-inspired western researchers were doing. Naturally, after the disintegration of the Soviet regime all this has changed for the better and in principle the free exchange of scientific ideas is now hampered only by economic factors. However, the traces of the historical situation are still among us and one can still distinguish different strands of neo-Vygotskian research based on nationality. Further distinctions within the Vygotsky-inspired research can be made on the basis of the specific topic selected for elaboration. Some researchers, for example, have focused on the idea of mediation, others on scientific concepts, still others on the zone of proximal development, and so on. The result is a bewildering variety of literally hundreds of neo-Vygotskian investigations. Naturally, in the pages that follow I cannot discuss even a fraction of this research.[1] Instead, I have opted to discuss a number of investigations that are clearly tied to a few of Vygotsky's major themes and concepts as presented in the preceding chapters.

One of these themes is that of the zone of proximal development. As we saw in Chapter 4, the concept of the zone of proximal development involved a number of ideas. The first idea is that cognitive functions develop in *cooperation* or *social interaction* with more able partners. That idea in itself triggers a number of questions that call for an answer. Obviously, Vygotsky meant to say that the child's intellectual abilities develop in cooperation that is somehow adequate, instructive or helpful. A first question might thus be what makes cooperation instructive. Further, we may ask who these more able partners are. For example, are we talking about parents or about teachers? And does that make a difference, i.e. do 'good' parents coach their children differently from good teachers? Finally, we may ask whether Vygotsky was actually right. Does it make a difference for the child's cognitive development whether the parent or teacher is 'good' from some point of view? Let us first have a look at some research that looks at the teaching strategies of parents.

Scaffolding

In the late 1970s Bruner and Wood introduced the notion of 'scaffolding'[2] to describe the temporary supporting activity of parents when they jointly solve a problem with their child. The parent may create certain 'formats', i.e. standard situations in which certain interactions invariably take place (Bruner 1983) – the parent may draw the child's attention to salient aspects of the task, the parent may parcel the task into easily manageable subtasks, and so on. It is a process of '"setting up" the situation to make the child's entry easy and successful and then gradually pulling back and handing the role to the child as he becomes skillful enough to manage it' (Bruner 1983, p. 60). Such a general strategy requires careful monitoring of the child's utterances and actions, and adjusting one's demands to their level. In a series of investigations, Wood (1980; Wood, Bruner and Ross 1976; Wood, Wood and Middleton 1978) and his colleagues investigated whether a parent's tutorial intervention should be inversely related to the child's level of task competence. They asked mothers to teach their three- to four-year-old children how to do a construction task and classified the mother's interventions into categories of increasing concreteness or explicitness. For example, unspecified verbal encouragement, such as the question 'What are you going to do now?', was classified as the least explicit form of intervention. A full demonstration, in which the mother essentially does part of the task, was classified as the most explicit form of instruction. In between were three levels of increasing explicitness or concreteness (e.g. 'Get the little blocks', 'Take that block over there and put it here'). Wood and his colleagues hypothesized that an ideal tutoring strategy might be to intervene at a level that is more explicit after the child makes an error and at a level that is less explicit when the child performs well. Thus, in their interventions the parents should go up and down the hierarchy of explicitness depending on the child's performance. The interesting thing is that such a tutorial strategy actually seemed to work. The correlation between the parents' tendency to follow this contingency rule and the child's subsequent ability to do the construction task independently was very high. Moreover, mothers who followed this strategy were also successful with other people's children (Wood 1980, pp. 286–7). The research done by Wood was important in that it empirically showed the transition from other-regulation to self-regulation posited by Vygotsky (see Chapters 3 and 4) and the effectiveness of a specific teaching strategy. As Wood (1980, p. 295) concluded, the effective parent-teacher operates 'in what Vygotsky called the child's zone of proximal development' (cf. McNaughton and Leyland 1999; Pratt et al. 1999).

Sensitivity

Wood's findings were also important in that they showed that parents follow teaching strategies with children who are much younger than the ones Vygotsky had in mind when talking about the zone of proximal development. In fact, other research has shown that adults have at their disposal a whole repertoire of techniques to lure very young children, including newborns, into the world of meaning and culture. Parents draw the child's attention by speaking with a high-pitched voice; they point out salient aspects of the environment through exaggerated gestures; they segment complex tasks into easier ones, and so on. In sum, very many data have been gathered that confirm Vygotsky's claim that individual cognitive (intrapsychological) processes emerge in and through the continual interaction with adults or more able peers of their culture (interpsychological processes) (cf. Butterworth and Grover 1999; Dunn 1988; Kaye 1982; Light 1979; Schaffer 1984; Stern 1985).

Interestingly, the tutorial strategies that parents practice seem to be inseparable from the affective processes that also take place during interaction. Children are not just in need of all the cognitive support they can get; they also benefit from encouragement and praise (Kozulin 2003). Moreover, the child's confidence needed to explore and investigate the environment independently benefits from a secure emotional bond with a parent. According to attachment theory, such a secure bond develops when the parent carefully monitors the child's behavior and promptly reacts to the child's signals. In other words, when the parent is emotionally sensitive (Ainsworth 1967). Elsewhere (Van der Veer and Van Ijzendoorn 1988, p. 224), I have argued that the basic processes of sensitive responsiveness in the affective and the cognitive domain have much in common (cf. Meins 1999). In both domains careful monitoring of the child's current abilities, signals, or states of mind is indispensable. In both domains the parent should adjust to the child's point of view in order to reach common understanding (the asymmetry condition). Finally, in both domains the caregiver will make demands on the child when he or she feels the child is ready for it (the contingency rule). From this point of view, the relationship between adult and child is regarded as an asymmetrical one, despite the active and often creative role of the child. It is the adult who has the burden of the responsibility; it is the parent who slowly and carefully introduces the infant into the cultural world and thereby makes the child's cognitive development possible.

Thus, modern research has basically corroborated Vygotsky's view that the child's cognitive processes develop in social interaction with adults or more able peers. At the same time, it turned out that the picture is incredibly complex. Social interaction may take an infinite variety of forms and it lasts from when the child is born until far into adolescence. In this fundamentally asymmetrical relationship the child is introduced to the cultural tools of his or her society. However, there is more to child development than just cognition. Attachment theorists have shown that a secure affective relationship with one or more adults forms at least a pre-condition for adequate cognitive development to take place. In that respect, Vygotsky's theory may have been overly rational in its emphasis on (the stimulation of) cognitive development and may benefit from modern research into affective adult–child relationships.

Teaching in the Classroom: The Work of Gal'perin

It is one thing to investigate the alleged adequate tutoring strategies in joint problem solving by mother–child dyads, or their affective relationships. It is quite another issue to define effective teaching strategies for the classroom. In this area as well, many educational thinkers have felt inspired by Vygotsky's scattered ideas and, of course, they have concentrated on different aspects of his work. Among these thinkers a principal figure was Pyotr Gal'perin (1902–88), a former collaborator of Leontiev and Luria. Most important in this context is his so-called *theory of the stepwise formation of mental acts*, which aimed to elaborate Vygotsky's ideas about the internalization process and to provide a powerful instructional method. As we saw in Chapter 3, Vygotsky claimed that internal mental processes originate in and are modeled upon external processes. Gal'perin accepted this general idea, but he pointed out several issues in Vygotsky's theory that still had to be clarified. First, it was insufficiently clear how exactly the transition from external to internal aids takes place. Second, it was unclear what factors promote the transition from external to internal processes. Third, Vygotsky's and Leontiev's investigations (e.g. the forbidden colors task described in Chapter 3) were often cross-sectional studies, which made it impossible to trace the transition from external to internal processes *in vivo* in an individual. Fourth, Vygotsky did not succeed in developing a method for the systematic formation of internal processes (Haenen 1996, p. 121). Gal'perin's theory of the stepwise formation of mental acts was an attempt to address these issues making use of another of Vygotsky's ideas, namely about the origin and function of inner speech.

In its final form, Gal'perin's theory said that in order to master a certain skill properly, the child must be guided through a number of stages. First, the child must be amply familiarized with the task at hand and be introduced to the operations that lead to task completion. Second, the child must first practice these operations in a material or materialized way while speaking aloud. For example, when learning to add, the child must first practice addition and subtraction by adding and removing toy cows and stating 'Two cows plus one cow makes three cows'. Third, this material stage should be followed by a stage in which the children are encouraged to drop the material manipulation, but to retain the speech that accompanied it. At first they may speak aloud, but gradually they are encouraged to switch to whispering to themselves and finally to inner speech. The great advantage of resorting to mere speech rather than to material manipulation plus speech is, of course, that speech can be applied much more generally (e.g. the sentence 'Two cows plus one cow makes three cows' is valid for all cows, not just for the toy ones the subject has been manipulating). Similarly, the sentence 'Two plus one makes three' is valid for all objects (and not just for cows) and much faster than concrete manipulation. Finally, after sufficient practice the operations will be carried out more smoothly, inner speech will become abbreviated and the children will have reached the stage of pure thought or, in Gal'perin's terms, the stage of mental actions.

One can easily see that this theory joins several of Vygotsky's concepts discussed earlier. For example, the idea that in child development external mediation precedes internal mediation is combined with the idea that inner speech originates in external and egocentric speech and has a regulating function. Moreover, when Gal'perin and his co-workers implemented this theory in concrete teaching programs (e.g. teaching mathematical concepts) they linked up with the notion of scientific concepts. However, Gal'perin's theory is much more concrete and elaborate than Vygotsky's original suggestions. He also introduced certain characteristics (e.g. the emphasis on strict guidance of the learner, the need to avoid mistakes by the learner, the necessity of material manipulation) that have led to much discussion in the Russian and international scientific press (Haenen 1996; Rahmani 1973; Van der Veer 2000). The empirical question, whether children who are taught according to a Gal'perin-type instructional program perform better than other children, cannot be definitively answered at this moment. Gal'perin and his followers have claimed spectacular results (e.g. deep understanding of the subject, good transfer), but just like in the case of dynamic assessment (see below) these claims need to be evaluated and replicated in careful empirical research. It is not too early, however, to state that Gal'perin's theory is highly interesting and that his method of the stepwise formation of mental acts is one of the more serious candidates for a didactical approach in well-defined areas of knowledge (Arievitch and Stetsenko 2000). What Gal'perin provided was a concrete elaboration of several of Vygotsky's rather general notions about the relationship between instruction and development and this is in itself no small feat.

Teaching in the Classroom: Scientific Concepts

Although Gal'perin's approach is interesting, other researchers have looked for different leads in the work of Vygotsky and his students (see Daniels 2001; Kozulin et al. 2003; Moll 1990). Marianne Hedegaard and Seth Chaiklin (2005), for example, have taken inspiration from ideas that were elaborated by the Russian researchers El'konin (a student of Vygotsky) and Davydov. El'konin and Davydov argued that the essential relations in a domain of knowledge (e.g. mathematics, history) can be captured by abstract models that should be introduced fairly early in education to act as organizing principles that connect the otherwise seemingly disconnected parts of the subject matter. A model depicting the forces operative in evolution, for example, can explain many phenomena in biology. With the help of such models the children can ideally understand phenomena they have not yet encountered in school subjects and in their own life. El'konin's and Davydov's ideas have been tested in many classrooms both inside and outside Russia with promising results and Hedegaard and Chaiklin (2005) decided to apply this approach in the Puerto Rican community in Harlem, New York, where many children do not perform well in the educational system. How to get these children motivated and to improve their academic results? The authors decided to carry out a small-scale teaching experiment in an after-school program. The pupils were 15 children of 8 to 12 years old who met 37 times with a frequency of about twice a week. They joined 'The Young Scientist's Club', which focused on three research areas: the conditions of life in Puerto Rico in the early twentieth century, the living conditions of Puerto Rican immigrants in New York in that same period and the living conditions of the present Puerto Rican community in East Harlem. The idea was that the children would have local, everyday knowledge about these topics and that they could be easily motivated to study them further, which would lead to an enriched understanding of their own background and situation. As the authors argued, 'The teacher who wants pupils to learn and appropriate knowledge and skills that can transcend the classroom activities and influence their everyday activities, must engage, build upon, and develop the pupil's personal everyday knowledge' (Hedegaard and Chaiklin 2005, p. 66). Hedegaard and Chaiklin introduced a core model that depicted the basic relations between family, community, resources, and living conditions and introduced the children to the scientific way of thinking (e.g. What do we want to know? How do we get to know it? Which results did we find? What do these results mean? And so on). Armed with the core model and the scientific approach the children set out to explore their research topics. What Hedegaard and Chaiklin found was that the children showed a growing understanding of crucial relationships during classroom discussions, that they proved able to use models, that they were more or less engaged, and that they reached a new understanding for and appreciation of their local community and their relation to it. In itself that is no small accomplishment for a group of children who do not do very well in the regular educational system. Hedegaard's and Chaiklin's investigation deserves to be replicated on a larger scale and with traditional outcome measures (cf. Van der Veer 2006).

The teaching experiment by Hedegaard and Chaiklin is just one of the many dozens of Vygotsky-inspired investigations that have taken place over the last few decades. And if we compare it with Gal'perin's approach described above we get a glimpse of the bewildering variety of these investigations. Some researchers focus on the necessity of material manipulation and subsequent verbalization; others make use of abstract models and charts that guide the children's thinking process; still others focus on frequent classroom discussions, and so on. Clearly, under the umbrella of Vygotsky-inspired educational theory, the research is branching off in different directions.

From School to Life: Literacy

Above we have seen that Vygotsky and Luria attributed enormous significance to the acquisition of literacy. Becoming able to read and write constitutes a major step in the child's semiotic development that is prepared by various previous activities in the child's life (Vygotsky 1929/1935). In conversation, children learn to use certain gestures to convey meaning. In symbolic play, they learn to use objects as if they were another object or a person. In drawing, they learn to refer to objects by pictorial means. In Vygotsky's analysis, all these abilities form part of an incredibly complex *semiotic* development. What children learn is to use conventional tools or signs (e.g. gestures, objects, drawings) to refer to something else. Learning to write is only possible on the basis of these previous developments and forms its culmination point. Specific for writing is that the child must analyze the sound structure of words and convey them with letters. Moreover, writing messages to another person makes demands on a child that are rather special. In Chapter 4 we have seen that Vygotsky concluded that literacy leads to insight or reflection and to conscious or deliberate control.

Vygotsky's reasoning was most interesting, but the data he adduced were rather vague or anecdotal. The expedition to Uzbekistan (Chapter 5) could not solve this problem, because it suffered from various methodological problems. As we have seen, Luria's subjects varied in their involvement in new societal structures, their degree of schooling and their degree of literacy. Luria could not possibly vary these factors independently and hence he could not measure the effect of literacy per se. However, it is important to distinguish between the effects of, say, schooling and literacy. It has been argued that certain activities in western school (e.g. discussing topics from different viewpoints, presenting subject matter outside of its normal context) may lead to the ability to think abstractly and hypothetically that Luria found in some of his Uzbek subjects. Thus, the cognitive effects that Vygotsky attributed to literacy may in reality be due to certain school practices.

Fortunately, under certain exceptional circumstances it is possible to tease apart these effects somewhat further. Some 25 years ago, Scribner and Cole (1981) published the results of an extensive study – inspired by Vygotsky's cultural-historical theory – that addressed exactly this issue. The study was conducted in Liberia where the Vai, a small West African group, have developed their own syllabic writing system (cf. Leroy 1927). The important thing is that this Vai script is not taught in school, but in the home, and is primarily used for the purpose of letter-writing to relatives. Part of the Vai population attends an English-language school. Another part of the population attends a *madrassah*, where they learn, among other things, to memorize the Qur'an. Finally, part of the population attends no school and remains illiterate. Scribner and Cole tested the cognitive effects of this checkered pattern of school systems and literacies by submitting their Vai participants to a variety of tests (not unlike those used by Luria, but more elaborate and more sophisticated). Their general finding was that persons excelled on tasks that were similar to those they had been practicing. For example, Vai literates performed well on a task that tapped the abilities needed for letter-writing (e.g. explaining the rules of a game to an outsider); students who participated in a *madrassah* were good at incremental recall tasks; and subjects attending the English school were proficient in all sorts of tasks that require verbal exposition or explanation (Scribner and Cole 1981, pp. 242–55). Thus, Scribner and Cole were able to show that literacy makes a difference, but that, more than literacy per se (as a coding-decoding skill), it is the different practices to which it is put that yield the important cognitive differences. Moreover, school yielded the most cognitive effects, which points to the fact that certain school practices (e.g. debating topics in a group, asking a person to explain his point of view) may be important for cognitive development.

The Liberia study confirmed Vygotsky's and Luria's findings in that it convincingly showed that there are measurable differences in the cognitive performance ('higher psychological functions') of people who come from a different cultural background. However, it also showed that the cognitive effects of literacy per se are modest as compared to the effects of certain activities practiced both inside and outside of school. In itself, these findings may be compatible with the spirit of Vygotsky's thinking. Clearly, when he stressed the importance of learning to read and write (letters, in particular) he was not thinking about coding-decoding skills but about the fact that this skill would lead the child to *think* about and *understand* his or her own language, just like learning algebra makes the child aware of certain principles that he or she had applied in arithmetic all the time without giving them a thought (Vygotsky 1934a).[3] What Vygotsky did not see is that literacy as such has no unequivocal influence on cognitive functioning, that not every type of literacy leads to major cognitive changes as one can teach literacy (and numeracy) as narrow technical skills. Kozulin (2003) has argued that Scribner's and Cole's findings raise the question under what specific circumstances mediators become tools of thinking with a general transformatory power. They also raise the question of which practices in the western school other than the mastering of literacy, numeracy, and so on, produce the cognitive effects found and whether formal school instruction is superior to informal socialization in any general way.

Formal and Informal Schooling

To Vygotsky there was no doubt that children need instruction, that the best instruction is given in school, that the academic knowledge acquired at school pervades the child's thinking, and that it is relevant for life outside school. Subsequent research, however, has called into doubt several of these beliefs. For example, it has proved surprisingly difficult to find large cognitive differences between children who did and who did not attend school. After much research, Scribner and Cole (1981, p. 252) concluded that the available data 'caution us against considering literacy and schooling as the only vehicles for the promotion of the cognitive skills we have studied'. They suggest, for example, urban residency as an additional potentially relevant factor. Another point is that of transfer: contrary to Vygotsky's expectations, skills learned at school may not be applied in everyday life. One of the surprising results of Scribner's and Cole's investigation was indeed that it is so difficult to find examples of transfer of learning, i.e. persons do not seem to routinely generalize the academic knowledge learned at school to everyday life tasks. Thus, the difference between schooled and non-schooled subjects may be attenuated by the fact that (a) cognitive skills can also be acquired outside school and by (b) a lack of transfer from school knowledge to everyday life. Both of these options have been discussed in the work of Jean Lave (1988; Lave and Wenger 1991) and Barbara Rogoff (1990; 2003).

Lave participated as a researcher in Scribner and Cole's Liberia study (see Chapter 5) and started off where that investigation ended. Her primary goal has been to study everyday cognition as a form of situationally specific cognitive activity. Lave studied the use of arithmetic in everyday life and found results that contradicted widely held assumptions. Thus, adults do not routinely apply the algorithms learned at school in everyday life, nor do successful and unsuccessful learners differ in this respect. Rather, they invent their own situationally specific rules. Moreover, Lave found that everyday arithmetic is not inferior to school arithmetic, but rather qualitatively different.

Lave (1988, p. 65) cites the following example of a Brazilian coconut seller, who learned at school to multiply a number by ten by placing a zero to the right of that number, but who nevertheless invented his own routine.

CUSTOMER: How much is one coconut?
SELLER: 35
CUSTOMER: I'd like ten. How much is that?
SELLER: (Pause) Three will be 105; with three more, that will be 210. (Pause) I need four more. That is ... (pause) ... I think it is 350.

Such results led Lave to reject thinking about scientific and everyday thinking in terms of a dichotomy, a dichotomy she traces back to the distinction between primitive and western thinking made by, among others, Lévy-Bruhl (Lave 1988, p. 78), and that, as we have seen, was shared by Vygotsky.

Just like Lave, Rogoff has stressed that cognition is a socially situated activity that can take various forms. In her view, the role of explicit verbal instruction as a socializing agent has been overemphasized. Children often learn by observation, eavesdropping, and by what she calls guided participation.

> Guided participation involves collaboration and shared understanding in routine problem-solving activities. Interaction with other people assists children in their development by guiding their participation in relevant activities, helping them adapt their understanding to new situations, structuring their problem-solving attempts, and assisting them in assuming responsibility for managing problem solving. This guidance of development includes tacit and intuitive forms of communication and distal arrangements of children's learning environments; it is often not designed for the instruction of children and may not involve contact or conversation. The model is one of routine arrangements and engagements that guide children's increasingly skilled and appropriate participation in the daily activities valued in their culture.
> (Rogoff 1990, p. 191)

Obviously, Rogoff here moves away from the idea of school instruction as the major agent in producing cognitive changes in children.

The idea of school as the provider of abstract rational language-based knowledge to be applied in a variety of everyday contexts she replaces by the metaphor of apprenticeship: children often learn by participating in activities guided by more able partners and by observing them. During these activities they appropriate culturally relevant information and skills, which they creatively transform at the same time (cf. Lave and Wenger 1991; Wenger 1998).

Both Lave's and Rogoff's insights are relevant for our evaluation of Vygotsky's thinking about education and cognitive development. On the basis of their own cross-cultural investigation of everyday thinking they reached positions that call into doubt several of Vygotsky's beliefs. First, the mutual enrichment of scientific and everyday concepts may not easily occur, i.e. the abstract rational type of thinking taught in school doesn't easily spread to other contexts. Second, there is no need to regard everyday thinking as necessarily inferior: all forms of thinking develop in specific cultural practices and are fit for them. Third, in many societies important knowledge and skills are not primarily transmitted verbally in school, but through observation of and guided participation in shared activities. Taken together and if proven true, these claims would somewhat undermine Vygotsky's emphasis on the importance of literacy and schooling for cognitive development. They are, however, entirely in accord with Vygotsky's more general position that cognitive development is largely a process of mastering cultural tools guided by more able social others.

The Dynamic Assessment of Intelligence

As we have seen, the concept of the zone of proximal development also involved the idea that we can determine the child's *learning potential*. That is, Vygotsky claimed that with the dual testing procedure we can get a better indication of the child's future performance in some domain. Obviously, we can ask whether this claim stands for truth and investigate whether the dual assessment procedure indeed yields a better prediction of, for example, school results than ordinary mental testing. Further, Vygotsky spoke of giving the child hints and prompts, showing part of the solution, and so on. However, he did not specify how exactly this should be done. The question, then, is whether we can work out standardized ways to provide assistance that guarantee that one child does not get more assistance than another. Or, we may decide to use the amount of help received in reaching some criterion as an index for the child's learning potential. Another question is whether we view the joint testing period as a means to explore and diagnose the child's genuine potential or whether we regard it as a learning phase. That is, we may consider the hints and prompts given as some form of instruction that boosts the child's IQ. But do children necessarily perform better when they get help or might it be the other way around for some children? These and other issues are now being explored in the burgeoning field of dynamic assessment and the outlines of different approaches and some preliminary answers are gradually emerging. Grigorenko and Sternberg (1998; Sternberg and Grigorenko 2002) have recently reviewed much of the dynamic assessment literature. Their ultimate conclusion is that the field of dynamic assessment is promising, but that many investigations still fail to meet the demands of rigorous standards of empirical research. Careful replication research is needed to determine the truth-value of the claims advanced by the researchers in this field. To give an impression of the relevant research I shall briefly discuss three different approaches.

The graduated-prompts approach

The graduated-prompts approach was developed by Campione and Brown (Campione 1989; Campione and Brown 1987) and combines several of Vygotsky's ideas, although their actual procedure differs. Unlike Vygotsky, these authors do not provide hints and prompts and then establish how far the joint test score exceeds the child's individual test score. Instead, they measure how many hints and prompts the child requires to solve a specified problem. It is assumed that children with much potential profit more from the intervention and need less assistance. Interestingly, they also focus on the issue of learning transfer, i.e. they check whether the child can apply newly acquired skills to problems they haven't seen before (see Chapters 4 and 5). Their full procedure is as follows: (a) it is established how well the child performs individually; (b) the child receives predetermined hints that range from general to specific (cf. Wood's procedure described above) until he or she can solve the problems independently (e.g. when two consecutive problems have been solved without assistance); (c) the child is again tested individually on both similar problems and problems that differ somewhat (near transfer) or differ widely (far transfer); (d) the child receives hints when solving similar and different problems. Brown and Campione establish the number of prompts received by the child and the child's ability to solve similar and (very) different problems. These are combined into an individual score that supposedly reflects the child's learning potential. Brown and Campione worked with various groups of children (children with learning disabilities, non-mentally impaired and mildly mentally impaired children) and with a variety of tasks (e.g. series-completion, reading). In a series of investigations, they found that children with higher IQ scores require less help to master similar and transfer problems, which is not a very surprising finding. Somewhat more unexpected is that older children require less coaching than younger children. This suggests that the ability to profit from experience in itself develops as one grows older. Brown and Campione and researchers who have employed their paradigm found that the predictive power of their own measures was higher than that of traditional IQ scores, i.e. measuring the amount of assistance needed and the number of transfer problems solved yields better information as to who will do well in school (or on new problems) than traditional static IQ tests. Moreover, they found that on the basis of their procedure they could distinguish between different groups of weak students: learning disabled children needed significantly less assistance than mildly mentally impaired children. This is an important diagnostic finding that we come across repeatedly in the dynamic assessment literature. Unlike the traditional static IQ measures, the new procedures allow one to distinguish between those who can and those who cannot profit from instruction in the form of hints and prompts. That finding reminds us of the distinction introduced by Petrova (1925) and Vygotsky between 'primitive' and 'feeble-minded' children and their alleged different prognosis. Thus, although much still remains to be done (cf. Grigorenko and Sternberg 1998, pp. 38–9), the findings of the researchers working in the tradition of Campione and Brown suggest that this approach has both predictive and diagnostic value. In addition, it addresses the vital issue of the transfer of learning.

The work of Budoff

Just like Vygotsky, Budoff proceeds from the assumption that traditional static IQ tests underestimate the abilities of various groups of disadvantaged children. Children who lack a proper education, children from other cultures and learning-disabled children run the risk of unfair classification on the basis of the traditional testing approach. Budoff adjusted a number of traditional tests (e.g. the *Raven's Progressive Matrices*) and coined them *Budoff's Measures of Learning Potential* (e.g. Budoff 1987a; 1987b). Typically, the child is first tested individually (the pretest). Then follows a training stage during which the child is coached and encouraged to solve the problems. Just as in the work of Wood, and Campione and Brown, assistance becomes more concrete after failure. Finally, the child is again individually tested in the traditional way (the post-test). On the basis of their pretest and post-test scores Budoff and his colleagues distinguished between three groups of disadvantaged children: (a) those who performed well initially and without help (*high scorers*); (b) those who initially scored low, but improved significantly after training (*gainers*); and (c) those who initially scored low and did not improve with training (*non-gainers*). This procedure is different from that of Campione and Brown's in that it characterizes children in terms of gains in test scores and not in amount of help received. The procedure is different from the one suggested by Vygotsky in that it ends with an individual post-test. Budoff and his colleagues found that *gainers* do better at school than *non-gainers* and that dynamic scores predict academic achievement better than traditional IQ scores. Budoff has suggested that the *gainers* are educationally disadvantaged (culturally deprived) children, whereas the *non-gainers* may be mentally impaired (biologically impaired), and thus once again referred to the distinction between 'primitive' and 'feeble-minded' children mentioned above. Budoff also tried to distinguish between *gainers* and *non-gainers* on the basis of other characteristics (e.g. one group may be more motivated than the other), but these results are rather difficult to interpret. Grigorenko and Sternberg (1998, p. 33) concluded that Budoff's measures 'are fairly robust instruments for the restricted specific purpose of differentiating the population of low-IQ children in order to conduct proper educational placement and to predict future performance'. Thus, the empirical results so far gathered indicate that Budoff's measures have both diagnostic and predictive value and may be fairer to certain groups of poorly performing children than traditional IQ tests.

The work of Feuerstein

Feuerstein began developing his ideas in Israel in the 1940s and 1950s. Just like the Soviet Union several decades earlier, the Israeli educational system was confronted with many persons (both children and adults) coming from a different culture. In the case of Israel, they were mostly Jews from North African countries and holocaust survivors. When tested with ordinary static IQ tests, many of these subjects scored miserably and on the basis of their test scores alone they would have been referred to special schools. However, just like Vygotsky several decades earlier, Feuerstein did not believe that these persons were beyond help. Rather, he attributed their poor performance to cultural deprivation and learned helplessness and set out to explore and remedy their deficiencies. Just like Binet, his fundamental belief was that intelligence is not a fixed, largely innate property, but can be improved by training. The higher cognitive skills essential for intelligent functioning can be transmitted to the child by a skilled teacher or psychologist, called a *mediator*. Over the years, Feuerstein developed both an assessment instrument (LPAD) and an intervention program (IE) to be used in educational settings. The *Learning Potential Assessment Device* (LPAD) is essentially a test battery consisting of adapted existing static tests (e.g. *Raven's Progressive Matrices*) (cf. Budoff's measures). The battery was originally meant as a testing device for low-achieving children (notably, the immigrant children mentioned above), but has subsequently been used for normal achievers as well. The tests (or part of them) are administered in a flexible, individualized and interactive process that is designed to promote what Feuerstein calls a *mediated learning experience* (MLE).

During this process, the psychologist attempts to lay bare cognitive deficits and to find the proper instructions, hints and prompts for this particular child. However, the psychologist's role is not that of a neutral examiner: he also supports and encourages the child, and the whole setting is more like a sympathetic clinical interview. The goal is to both support and teach the child, and to assess his or her cognitive modifiability, that is, to what extent the child has been able to profit from the psychologist's coaching. On the basis of such an assessment it may be deemed necessary to take part in an intervention program, called the *Instrumental Enrichment* (IE) program. The goal of this program is to teach children thinking skills that can be flexibly applied in a variety of circumstances. The IE materials cover such areas as comparison, categorization and the use of syllogisms. They are designed to be content-free, process-oriented and systematically organized (Kozulin 2003). Much use is made of symbolic devices such as graphs and charts (cf. the work of Gal'perin) and the same principles reappear in different instruments in different modalities. In essence, the IE program strives to accomplish the metacognitive skills that Vygotsky thought would be the result of training in scientific concepts: awareness and control. And it does so by explicitly teaching different heuristics that can be applied in a variety of contexts. Hence, the student who has followed the program should be able to tackle many of the problems offered at school.

The work of Feuerstein is highly interesting; he and his colleagues have claimed important successes, and from a moral point of view their work is highly commendable. Yet, from the viewpoint of the pedantic methodologist one can make a few cautionary remarks. For example, Feuerstein and his colleagues have found that children who take (part of the) LPAD improve their scores, i.e. they score higher on some post-tests than on the pretest. In itself, however, such a result is not very spectacular: ever since people began using mental tests it has been demonstrated that test scores are susceptible to training. Also, further analysis of such results is needed to rule out testing effects, to determine whether possible effects are due to the person of the mediator or due to the method itself, and so on. Feuerstein and colleagues also found that the highest gains were demonstrated by those children who initially scored lowest, which suggests that his method is highly effective in remedying cultural deficits. However, it should first be ruled out that such improved scores are not wholly or partly due to regression effects (cf. Chapter 4, note 17). Feuerstein and his group are interested in achieving changes in the intellectual functioning of the child and do not believe that school results should be the ultimate judge on this account. Hence, they have expressed reservations against using school results as a criterion for the evaluation of the predictive validity of Feuerstein's test battery. Still, some researchers have tried to do exactly this. Shochet (see Grigorenko and Sternberg 1998, p. 23) found that children who gained more from the LPAD showed better subsequent performance at school. That would mean that the LPAD, just like Budoff's measures, is able to distinguish between *gainers* and *non-gainers* (or, in Feuerstein's terms, between children with high and low cognitive modifiability) and that this distinction is relevant for placement decisions. Unfortunately, Shochet's investigation is not without its methodological problems and does not allow us to make strong claims (see Grigorenko and Sternberg 1998, p. 23).

Thus, the available empirical research suffers from a number of methodological shortcomings and so far we cannot draw any definitive conclusions as to the success of Feuerstein's approach. However, this is true of much of the research in the social sciences and these sobering methodological remarks should not blind us to the potential value of Feuerstein's approach. It does seem true that with sustained and considerable effort one can enable poor learners to get more confidence, to handle cognitive problems better and to obtain better scores on traditional measures. It is a matter of educational policy or politics whether one is prepared to invest the time and money to help these students. The least one can say is that Feuerstein (like other dynamic testers) has shown that traditional static tests do not tell the whole story and that it would be unfair to determine a child's future on the basis of such tests.[4] He too found that some children can respond more to coaching than others, which in itself is a finding of diagnostic value. Finally, his IE program certainly seems a good program to instill general thinking skills in children.

The field of dynamic testing has grown much over the past 25 years and certainly seems to hold promise for the future. Its history is as yet insufficiently explored but above we have seen that Vygotsky is generally regarded as one of the founding fathers of the dynamic testing approach. His goal was to offer individual children the most challenging instruction by determining the lower and upper boundaries of their performance. This focus on individual children has been somewhat lost in the modern research, possibly because it would be so time consuming if realized.[5] Instead, many dynamic testers have focused on different groups of initially poorly performing children, such as immigrant children, children with learning disabilities, and so on. In testing these children they found that some children responded better to their hints and prompts than others and introduced a dichotomy that was present in Vygotsky's work as well, namely that between *gainers* and *non-gainers*, between *modifiable* and *non-modifiable* children, between *culturally deprived* and *organically impaired* children, in sum between those children who are more and those who are less responsive to teaching. Vygotsky suggested that culturally deprived children would benefit from schooling (notably, literacy), but did not discuss any special measures to assist them. Feuerstein and others have developed enrichment programs to enable these children to develop the thinking skills that will ultimately lead them to the *osoznanie* (conscious realization) and *ovladenie* (mastery) that Vygotsky saw as the product of schooling. The enrichment programs that have been developed to improve the thinking of *all* students (cf. Feuerstein) have nothing to do with using dynamic testing as a diagnostic device, but are in line with Vygotsky's general idea that teaching should lead development. In that sense they can be compared to the work of Gal'perin (see above), who also attempted to demonstrate that careful teaching can lead to results that are considerably better than we are used to.

Conclusions

In the preceding paragraphs we have seen many examples of research inspired by Vygotsky and his students. What they have in common is that the researchers subscribe to the notion that cognitive development is a process of mastering cultural tools under the guidance or supervision of other members of that culture. In a sense, that formulation may be misleading in that it suggests that the child's role is not creative and that the transmission of culture is a one-way process. We do know, however, that children often creatively change the cultural messages they appropriate and create their own world of meanings. Parents and teachers may not always realize it, but there is much to be learned from children. For this reason, modern researchers have emphasized the active and creative role of children in the acculturation process (Valsiner 2000). Nevertheless, the focus on the acquisition of existing cultural tools (without substantially changing them) is understandable, because the adult–child relationship is asymmetrical in that the child must still master all the cultural knowledge and skills the adult takes for granted.

From the common conviction that cognitive development involves the mastering of cultural tools under the guidance of other members of one's culture the theoretical orientations branch off into various directions. Some researchers have focused on guidance by the social other: it is another person who assists the child in his or her mastering of cultural tools and this person can act more or less adequately. Here we have come across such notions as scaffolding, sensitivity and apprenticeship. Other researchers have focused on the notion of the cultural tool as such. What cultural tools are most effective? What is the power of the cultural tools that Vygotsky favored? Here we can situate the research in the cognitive effects of literacy and many of the investigations that make use of the notions of scientific concepts, models and so on. Of course, many investigations have a mixed character and often the effects of the mediating person (whether his style of coaching or his personality) and the mediating tool cannot be distinguished any more than the effects of the therapist and the therapy on the patient. Still other investigations deal with the fit between child and cultural tool or between child and way of instruction. Here we can situate much of the dynamic assessment and cultural enrichment programs, where researchers try to develop means to assist particular groups of children so that they can reach levels of performance that are acceptable according to some standard.

Although we are far from reaching any definitive answers in any of the fields where Vygotsky's educational ideas are being explored and although much research is in need of replication, we can reach at least one rather simple conclusion: the whole field of Vygotskian–inspired research makes a surprisingly fresh impression. Different subdisciplines (e.g. dynamic assessment, cultural psychology) have sprouted and hundreds of articles have come out dealing with Vygotsky's educational ideas. Obviously, the Russian thinker from the 1930s still strikes a chord in modern educationalists. Their joint efforts to revive his thinking will come to the benefit of our profession and will eventually lead to Vygotsky's classification as a classical thinker whose ideas need to be interpreted anew by each new generation of researchers, just like we retranslate Tolstoy so that he can inspire a new generation of readers.

Chapter 7

Conclusions

Vygotsky developed his ideas about the relationship between instruction and development in the late 1920s and early 1930s. This was a period of worldwide enthusiastic experimentation with newer forms of teaching that were called 'progressive'. Some of these initiatives went back to the late nineteenth century; others were of more recent date. Of the more famous educational experiments we can mention the following. John Badley (1865–1967) founded the still existing Bedales School in the United Kingdom in 1893. A few years later, in 1896, the pragmatist philosopher John Dewey (1859–1952) began applying his educational philosophy in the Laboratory School at the University of Chicago. Maria Montessori (1870–1952) first implemented her educational ideas in the *Casa dei Bambini* in 1907 and throughout the 1920s and 1930s actively spread her ideas all over the world. After her split with Montessori in 1918, Helen Parkhurst (1857–1973) developed her own Dalton Plan system and founded the Dalton School. Peter Petersen (1854–1952), professor of education at Jena in Germany, developed the Jena Plan concept at an experimental school from 1924. The Austrian architect and Goethe scholar Rudolf Steiner (1861–1925) developed the concept of the anthroposophist Waldorf schools. The German pedagogue Georg Kerschensteiner (1854–1932) proposed the concept of the labor school (*Arbeitsschule*). Although these school reformers adhered to widely differing and at times mutually contradictory philosophies, one can distinguish a handful of ideas which most of them shared. Of course, they all abhorred the old school. The traditional school was viewed as an institution in which children were made unduly passive, forced to give ready-made answers to stereotyped questions. The knowledge that was spread in traditional schools was abstract and divorced of any practical relevance. The new schools emphasized that children were unique human beings who could independently and at their own pace acquire new knowledge both in and outside school. Efforts were made to bring society into school or school into society. Teachers with their pupils visited factories and roamed through nature to discover the practical relevance of such subjects as mathematics, biology, physics and chemistry *in situ*. Often, a one-sided emphasis on abstract learning was prevented by having children do manual tasks such as carpentry, cooking, or tending a garden. The new schools were to be child oriented, democratic and concerned with the concrete problems of everyday life. While many of these experiments did not last, they left a significant trace in Western education and many of the educational ideas that today are presented or viewed as 'new 'and 'cutting edge' (e.g. Sudbury Valley School in the USA) essentially repeat those of the late nineteenth and early twentieth century.

Naturally, this wave of progressive educational ideas did not pass by the Soviet Union. The philosopher Pavel Blonsky, for example, was strongly influenced by John Dewey's educational philosophy of 'learning by doing' and proposed his own version of a labor school (Kozulin 1984). The goal of these schools was to introduce the children to contemporary industrial culture. Children were to work in concrete real-life projects to master the principles of science. Education should start by acquainting the children with their immediate surroundings with the emphasis on factories and firms. Like in other progressive approaches the ideal was the all-sided or polytechnic development of the personality (see Chapter 2). Blonsky's ideas were initially favorably received by the leading persons within the educational system, such as Nadezhda Krupskaya, and attempts were made to implement his and others' educational ideas. However, the desperate economic and social conditions of the Soviet Union in the 1920s frustrated many experiments with progressive schools and by the early 1930s the ideological climate had already changed (Kozulin 1984). Now all progressive educational initiatives were condemned as 'leftist deviations'. Different decrees ordered the abolition of progressive schools and by the late 1930s no trace was left of them.

Soviet education had become traditional again. Kozulin has argued that progressive education and the totalitarian Soviet system were in the end irreconcilable:

> Progressivism was based on the principle of democracy in education, whereas the Party leadership was proclaiming the dictatorship of the proletariat; and progressivism was committed to the idea of experimental projects that were hardly welcome in the more and more centralized system of Soviet public education, which required a stereotyped curriculum for all schools.
> (Kozulin 1984, pp. 133–4)

There is no doubt that Vygotsky was well aware of these new developments in the educational system. He was a student of Blonsky's (see Chapter 1), he was closely involved with the leading figures at the Ministry of Education and he had himself been teaching at all levels of education. When writing about the zone of proximal development he contrasted that concept with the concept of 'sensitive period' introduced by Montessori (cf. Droogleever Fortuyn 1924) claiming that his was a social concept whereas Montessori's concept was biological (Vygotsky 1934a, pp. 222–3). Elsewhere, he extensively discussed Montessori's method of teaching writing (Vygotsky 1929/1935, pp. 90–4). So, it seems obvious that Vygotsky knew of most of the educational experiments that were going on both inside and outside the Soviet Union. But if we accept that claim, then the question might arise why Vygotsky did not formulate a plan for educational reforms himself. Isn't it strange that Vygotsky, one of the most influential educational thinkers of our time, never proposed concrete ideas for the new school in the final years of his career? In my view, there are three partial answers to that question. First, there was the political situation sketched above. In the early 1930s, any educational plan that deviated from the traditional system had become a 'leftist deviation' and even Krupskaya, Lenin's widow, was forced to recant her views on the issue of progressive education (Bauer 1952). Second, Vygotsky was not a pedagogue or educationalist by profession. He taught psychology and pedology, supervised psychological investigations carried out by his colleagues and students and worked as a clinical consultant. Third, and perhaps most important, Vygotsky did not intend to develop concrete ideas about the organization of schools, the development of curricula, and so on. Rather, in a sense, what he intended to do was to develop a theory of what it means to become a human person. What makes us human beings different from other animals? What is human development about? What makes us conscious persons? These were the fundamental questions that bothered Vygotsky and which he tried to answer with his cultural-historical theory of the higher mental functions (see Chapter 3). Vygotsky's goal was 'the creation of the *psychology of man*, the science of the complex laws of the human psyche', as Luria (1935, p. 224) wrote in his obituary. That fundamental goal also explains the general nature of his ideas. It was very rare that Vygotsky referred to concrete circumstances such as poverty, sex, social class, inadequate housing, bad school facilities, the hurly-burly of the classroom, and so on. Rather, he was talking about *the child* acquiring *the culture* of his parents. It is not surprising that in those times of militant communism this general nature of his ideas was used against him. As we have seen in Chapter 1, his Soviet critics chastised Vygotsky exactly for the lack of emphasis on issues such as social class and labor. In Marxist psychology 'the subject is never viewed as "man in general" but as the representative of a certain social class' (Borovsky 1929, p. 182). What the critics failed or refused to see was that Vygotsky's theory had the far-reaching and liberating consequences sketched in the previous chapters.

Perhaps the very fact that Vygotsky created a *general* view on the human developing child is another cause of his present popularity (cf. the Introduction) and the wildly varying nature of Vygotsky-inspired investigations. Perhaps hermetically closed theories that attempt to deal with each and every concrete detail of reality leave us little option: they must either be wholesale accepted or be discarded. The very fact of the general and unfinished nature of Vygotsky's theories may be their present strength. And the present-day psychologists and educationalists who work in the tradition of Vygotsky may be compared to the composers who attempt to complete Schubert's *Unfinished*. Part of the strength of Vygotsky's ideas is that they are open to the future.

Notes

1. Another question is what investigations can be legitimately considered to be neo-Vygotskian investigations. Obviously, it is impossible to draw clear-cut boundary lines, but I am convinced that Vygotsky would have disliked many papers that invoke his name. In this respect, Vygotsky has replaced Piaget, whose investigations and ideas were very fashionable in educational circles in the 1970s. In the following, I shall avoid any formal treatment of this issue (e.g. stipulating minimal criteria for Vygotskian research) and include only research that I personally consider genuinely Vygotskian.
2. Interestingly enough, Vygotsky and Luria (1930b, p. 202) once used the scaffolding notion to describe the development of locomotion. As they explained, the child who learns to walk is still holding on to chairs, tables, and so on, and in this sense his locomotion is in scaffolding for some time. As soon as the child has developed sufficiently strong muscles and adequate motor coordination he will discard this scaffolding and walk independently. Thus, Vygotsky and Luria introduced the notion of scaffolding as a temporary external support to be replaced by internal processes. Unfortunately, in the much praised English translation by Golod and Knox (Vygotsky and Luria 1993, p. 207) 'in scaffolding' is translated as 'to the woods', which doesn't make much sense to me.
3. 'Written speech indeed is the algebra of speech' (Vygotsky 1934a, p. 209).
4. The assumption that Western society needs as many subjects who have enjoyed what is called higher education as is possible (e.g. preferably a university education) can come at cross-purposes with the interests of individual children who have other preferences or abilities. What I mean is that children who have an outspoken interest in and excel in manual skills may easily be seen as academic failures if we focus exclusively on the teaching of abstract cognitive skills. Some form of polytechnic school (see Chapter 2), in which different learning routes are seen as variants rather than as levels of learning, might be preferable.

5. However, the massive availability of computers in classrooms now makes it in principle possible to measure the child's independent and joint performance in some area almost continually and to adjust the level of the tasks accordingly. That would ensure that the tasks offered to the child always lie in his or her zone of proximal development. Here, much depends on intelligent programming, although it seems to me that computers can never replace teachers.

Bibliography

Abel'skaya, R., and Neopikhonova, Y.S. (1932), 'Problema razvitiya v nemetskoy psikhologii i ee vliyanie na sovetskuyu pedologiyu i psikhologiyu'. *Pedologiya*, 4, 27–36.

Ageyev, V.S. (2003), 'Vygotsky in the mirror of cultural interpretations', in A. Kozulin, B. Gindis, V.S. Ageyev and S.M. Miller (eds), *Vygotsky's Educational Theory in Cultural Context*. Cambridge: Cambridge University Press, pp. 432–49.

Aikhenvald, Y.I. (1910), *Etyudy o Zapadnykh Pisatelyakh*. Moscow: Kostry.

Aikhenvald, Y.I. (1922), *Pokhvala Prazdnosti*. Moscow: Kostry.

Ainsworth, M.D. (1967). *Infancy in Uganda: Infant Care and the Growth of Love*. Baltimore: Johns Hopkins.

Arievitch, I.M., and Stetsenko, A.P. (2000), 'The quality of cultural tools and cognitive development: Gal'perin's contribution and its implications'. *Human Development*, 43, 69–92.

Balamore, U., and Wozniak, R.H. (1999), 'Speech-action coordination in young children', in P. Lloyd and C. Fernyhough (eds), *Lev Vygotsky: Critical Assessments. Vol. 2. Thought and Language*. London: Routledge, pp. 168–82.

Barash, D.P. (1986), *The Hare and the Tortoise: Culture, Biology and Human Nature*. Harmondsworth: Penguin.

Bauer, R.A. (1952), *The New Man in Soviet Psychology*. Cambridge, MA: Harvard University Press.

Benjamin, W. (1935/1972), 'Probleme der Sprachsoziologie: Ein Sammelreferat', in H. Tiedemann-Bartels (ed.), *Walter Benjamin. Gesammelte Schriften.Bd. III Kritiken und Rezensionen*. Frankfurt am Main: Suhrkamp Verlag, pp. 452–80.

Binet, A. (1911/1973), *Les Idées Modernes sur les Enfants*. Paris: Flammarion.

Binet, A., and Simon, T. (1905). 'Méthodes nouvelles pour le diagnostic du niveau intellectuel des anormaux'. *L'Année Psychologique*, 11, 191–244.

Bishop, O. (1924), 'What is measured by intelligence tests?'. *Journal of Educational Research*, 9, 29–38.

Blonsky, P.P. (1919/1979), 'Trudovaya shkola', in P.P. Blonsky, *Izbrannye Pedagogicheskie i Psikhologicheskie Sochineniya. Vol. 1*. Moscow: Pedagogika, pp. 86–164.

Boring, E.G. (1950), *A History of Experimental Psychology*. New York: Appleton-Century-Crofts.

Borovsky, V.M. (1929), 'Psychology in the U.S.S.R'. *Journal of General Psychology*, 2, 177–86.

Brill, R.G. (1984), *International Congress on Education of the Deaf: An Analytical History 1878–1980*. Washington, DC: Gallaudet College Press.

Brooks, S.S. (1922), 'Some uses for intelligence tests'. *Journal of Educational Research*, 5, 217–38.

Bruner, J. (1983), *Child's Talk: Learning to Use Language*. New York: Norton & Company.

Bruner, J. (1984), 'Vygotsky's zone of proximal development: The hidden agenda', in B. Rogoff and J.V. Wertsch (eds), *Children's Learning in the 'Zone of Proximal Development'*. San Francisco, CA: Jossey Bass, pp. 93–7.

Budoff, M. (1987a), 'The validity of learning potential', in C.S. Lidz (ed.), *Dynamic Testing*. New York: Guilford Press, pp. 52–81.

Budoff, M. (1987b), 'Measures for assessing learning potential', in C.S. Lidz (ed.), *Dynamic Testing*. New York: Guilford Press, pp. 173–95.

Bulanov, I. (1930), 'Materialy po izucheniyu povedeniya rebenka-tungusa'. *Pedologiya*, 1, 54–64.

Burks, B.S. (1928), *A Summary of Literature on the Determiners of the Intelligence Quotient and the Educational Quotient*. Bloomington, IL: The Public School Publishing Co.

Burt, C. (1927), *Mental and Scholastic Tests*. London: P.S. King and Son.

Butterworth, G., and Grover, L. (1999), 'The origins of referential communication in human infancy', in P. Lloyd and C. Fernyhough (eds), *Lev Vygotsky: Critical Assessments. Vol. 2. Thought and Language*. London: Routledge, pp. 3–22.

Campione, J.C. (1989), 'Assisted testing: A taxonomy of approaches and an outline of strengths and weaknesses'. *Journal of Learning Disabilities*, 22, 151–65.

Campione, J.C., and Brown, A. (1987), 'Linking dynamic testing with school achievement', in C.S. Lidz (ed.), *Dynamic Testing*. New York: Guilford Press, pp. 82–115.

Chaiklin, S. (2003), 'The zone of proximal development in Vygotsky's analysis of learning and instruction', in A. Kozulin, B. Gindis, V.S. Ageev and S.M. Miller (eds), *Vygotsky's Educational Theory in Cultural Context*. Cambridge: Cambridge University Press, pp. 65–82.

Chamberlain, L. (2006), *The Philosophy Steamer: Lenin and the Exile of the Intelligentsia*. London: Atlantic Books.

Cole, M. (1996). *Cultural Psychology: A Once and Future Discipline*. Cambridge, MA: The Belknap Press of Harvard University Press.

Cole, M. (2000), 'Struggling with complexity: The handbook of child psychology at the millennium'. *Human Development*, 43(6), 369–75.

Cole, M., and Cole, S. (1996), *The Development of Children* (3rd edn). New York: W.H. Freeman and Company.

Conquest, R. (1986), *The Harvest of Sorrow: Soviet Collectivization and the Terror-Famine*. Alberta: University of Alberta Press.

Coy, G.L. (1930), 'A study of various factors which influence the use of the accomplishment quotient as a measure of teaching efficiency'. *Journal of Educational Research*, 21, 29–42.

Daniels, H. (2001), *Vygotsky and Pedagogy*. New York: Routledge Falmer.

De Waal, F. (2001), *The Ape and the Shushi Master: Cultural Reflections of a Primatologist*. New York: Basic Books.

Droogleever Fortuyn, A.B. (1924), 'Sensitive periods'. *The Call of Education*, 1, 104–112.

Dunn, J. (1988), *The Beginnings of Social Understanding*. Oxford: Blackwell.

Efimov, V. (1931), 'Review of F.P. Petrov, Opyt issledovaniya intellektual'nogo razvitiya chuvashskikh detey po metodu Binet-Simon'. *Pedologiya*, 7–8, 127–8.

Engels, F. (1925), *Dialektik der Natur*. Berlin: Dietz Verlag.
Evans-Pritchard, E.E. (1934), 'Lévy-Bruhl's theory of primitive mentality'. *Bulletin of the Faculty of Arts*, 2. Cairo: Egyptian University.
Feigenberg, I.M. (ed.) (1996), *L.S. Vygotsky: Nachalo Puti*. Jerusalem: Jerusalem Publishing Centre.
Feofanov, M.P. (1932), 'Teoriya kul'turnogo razvitiya v pedologii kak elektricheskaya kontseptsiya, imeyushchaya v osnovnom idealicheskie korni'. *Pedologiya*, 1/2, 21–34.
Fordyce, C. (1921), 'Intelligence tests in classifying children in the elementary school'. *Journal of Educational Research*, 4, 40–3.
Gilbert, M. (1979), *The Jews of Russia*. Jerusalem: Bernstein.
Gornfeld, A.G. (1916), 'O tolkovanii khudozhestvennogo proizvedeniya'. *Voprosy Teorii i Psikhologii Tvorchestva*, 7, 1–30.
Gornfeld, A.G. (1923), 'D.N. Ovsyankino-Kulikovskiy i sovremennaya literaturnaya kritika'. *Voprosy teorii i Psikhologii Tvorchestva*, 8, 1–10.
Gould, S.J. (1981), *The Mismeasure of Man*. Harmondsworth: Penguin.
Grigorenko, E.L., and Sternberg, R.J. (1998), 'Dynamic testing'. *Psychological Bulletin*, 124, 75–111.
Haenen, J. (1996), *Piotr Gal'perin: Psychologist in Vygotsky's Footsteps*. Commack, NY: Nova Science Publishers.
Haggbloom, S.J., Warnick, R., Warnick, J.E., Jones, V.K., Yarbrough, G.L., Russell, T.M., Borecky, C.M., McGahhey, R., Powell, J.L., Beavers, J., and Monte, E. (2002), 'The 100 most eminent psychologists of the 20th century'. *Review of General Psychology*, 6, 139–52.
Hanfmann, E., and Kasanin, J. (1937), 'A method for the study of concept formation'. *Journal of Psychology*, 3, 521–40.
Hanfmann, E., and Kasanin, J. (1942), 'Conceptual thinking in schizophrenia'. *Journal of Nervous and Mental Diseases*, Monograph 67. New York: NMDM.
Hedegaard, M., and Chaiklin, S. (2005), *Radical-Local Teaching and Learning: A Cultural-Historical Approach*. Aarhus: Aarhus University Press.
Henmon, V.A.C. (1920), 'Improvement in school subjects throughout the school year'. *Journal of Educational Research*, 1, 81–95.
Hines, H.C. (1924), *A Guide to Educational Measurements*. Boston: Houghton Mifflin.

Jahoda, G. (1999), *Images of Savages: Ancient Roots of Modern Prejudice in Western Culture*. London: Routledge.

James, W. (1920), *Talks to Teachers*. London: Longmans, Green and Co.

Janet, P. (1928), *L'évolution de la Mémoire et de la Notion du Temps*. Paris: Chahine.

Joravsky, D. (1989), *Russian Psychology: A Critical History*. Oxford: Blackwell.

Kallom, A.W. (1922), 'Intelligence tests and the classroom teacher'. *Journal of Educational Research*, 5, 389–99.

Kasanin, J., and Hanfmann, F. (1938), 'An experimental study of concept formation in schizophrenia'. *American Journal of Psychiatry*, 95, 35–52.

Kaye, K. (1982), *The Mental and Social Life of Babies: How Parents Create Persons*. Chicago: University of Chicago Press.

Köhler, W. (1921). *Intelligenzprüfungen an Menschenaffen*. Berlin: Julius Springer.

Kornilov, K.N. (1928), 'The comparative value of research methods in psychology and pedology in light of Marxism'. *Psikhologiya*, 1, 5–27.

Kozulin, A. (1984), *Psychology in Utopia: Toward a Social History of Soviet Psychology*. Cambridge, MA: MIT Press.

Kozulin, A. (1990), *Vygotsky's Psychology: A Biography of Ideas*. New York: Harvester Wheatsheaf.

Kozulin, A. (2003), 'Psychological tools and mediated learning', in A. Kozulin, B. Gindis, V.S. Ageyev and S.M. Miller (eds), *Vygotsky's Educational Theory in Cultural Context*. Cambridge: Cambridge University Press, pp. 15–38.

Kozulin, A., Gindis, B., Ageyev, V.S., and Miller, S.M. (eds) (2003), *Vygotsky's Educational Theory in Cultural Context*. Cambridge: Cambridge University Press.

Kozyrev, A.V., and Turko, P.A. (1936), '"Pedagogicheskaya shkola" professora L.S. Vygotskogo'. *Vysshaya Shkola*, 2, 44–57.

Kurek, N. (2004), *Istoriya likvidatsii pedologii i psikhotekhniki*. St. Peterburg: Aleteyya.

Lashley, K.S. (1950), 'In search of the engram'. *Society of Experimental Biology*. Symposium 4, 454–82.

Lave, J. (1988), *Cognition in Practice*. Cambridge: Cambridge University Press.
Lave, J., and Wenger, E. (1991), *Situated Learning: Legitimate Peripheral Participation*. Cambridge: Cambridge University Press.
Leontiev, A.N. (1931), *Razvitie pamyati: Eksperimental'noe issledovanie vysshikh psikhologicheskikh funktsiy*. Moscow-Leningrad: Uchpedgiz.
Leontiev, A.N. (1932), 'Studies on the cultural development of the child (III): The development of voluntary attention in the child'. *Pedagogical Seminary and Journal of Genetic Psychology*, 40, 52–83.
Leroy, O. (1927), *La Raison Primitive: Essai de Refutation de la Théorie du Prélogisme*. Paris: Librairie Orientaliste Paul Geuthner.
Lévy-Bruhl, L. (1910/1922), *Les Functions Mentales dans les Sociétés Inférieures*. Paris: Alcan.
Lévy-Bruhl, L. (1922/1976), *La Mentalité Primitive*. Paris: Retz.
Lévy-Bruhl, L. (1949), *Les Carnets de Lucien Lévy-Bruhl*. Paris: PUF.
Lévy-Bruhl, L. (1966), *How Natives Think*. New York: Washington Square Press.
Lévy-Bruhl, L. (1975), *The Notebooks on Primitive Mentality*. Oxford: Blackwell.
Light, P.H. (1979), *The Development of Social Sensitivity*. Cambridge: Cambridge University Press.
Lloyd, P., and Fernyhough, C. (eds) (1999), *Lev Vygotsky: Critical Assessments* (4 volumes). London: Routledge.
Luria, A.R. (1928a), 'Psychology in Russia'. *Pedagogical Seminary and Journal of Genetic Psychology*, 35, 347–55.
Luria, A.R. (1928b), 'The problem of the cultural development of the child (I)'. *Pedagogical Seminary and Journal of Genetic Psychology*, 35, 493–506.
Luria, A.R. (1932a), 'Psychological expedition to Central Asia'. *Pedagogical Seminary and Journal of Genetic Psychology*, 40, 241–2.
Luria, A.R. (1932b), *The Nature of Human Conflicts: Or Emotion, Conflict and Will*. New York: Liveright Publishers.
Luria, A.R. (1934), 'The second psychological expedition to Central Asia'. *Pedagogical Seminary and Journal of Genetic Psychology*, 44, 255–9.
Luria, A.R. (1935), 'Professor L.S. Vygotsky (1896–1934)'. *Pedagogical Seminary and Journal of Genetic Psychology*, 46, 224–6.

Luria, A.R. (1973), *The Working Brain: An Introduction to Neuropsychology*. New York: Basic Books.
Luria, A.R. (1974), *Ob istoricheskom razvitii poznavatel'nykh protsessov*. Moscow: Nauka.
Luria, A.R. (1976), *Cognitive Development: Its Cultural and Social Foundations*. Cambridge, MA: Harvard University Press.
Luria, A.R. (1979), *The Making of Mind*. Cambridge, MA: Harvard University Press.
Luria, A.R. (1982), *Etapy proydennego put'i*. Moscow: Izdatel'stvo Moskovskogo Universiteta.
Luria, E.A. (1994), *Moi otets*. Moscow: Gnosis.
Mateer, F. (1918), 'The diagnostic fallibility of intelligence ratios'. *Pedagogical Seminary and Journal of Genetic Psychology*, 25, 369–92.
McCrory, J.R. (1932), 'The reliability of the accomplishment quotient'. *Journal of Educational Research*, 25, 27–39.
McLeish, J. (1975), *Soviet Psychology: History, Theory, Content*. London: Methuen & Co
McNaughton, S., and Leyland, J. (1999), 'The shifting focus of maternal tutoring across different difficulty levels on a problem-solving task', in P. Lloyd and C. Fernyhough (eds), *Lev Vygotsky: Critical Assessments. Vol. 3. The Zone of Proximal Development*. London: Routledge, pp. 132–42.
Medvedev, R.A. (1974), *K sudu istorii: Genezis i posledstviya Stalinizma*. New York: Alfred A. Knopf.
Meins, E. (1999), 'Security of attachment and maternal tutoring strategies: Interaction within the zone of proximal development', in P. Lloyd and C. Fernyhough (eds), *Lev Vygotsky: Critical Assessments. Vol. 3. The Zone of Proximal Development*. London: Routledge, pp. 113–31.
Melk-Koch, M. (1989), *Auf der Suche nach der Menschlichen Gesellschaft: Richard Thurnwald*. Berlin: Reimer.
Merton, R. (1968), 'The Matthew effect in science'. *Science*, 159 (3810), 56–63.
Meumann, E. (1914), *Vorlesungen zur Einfuhrung in die Experimentelle Padagogik. Bd. 2*. Leipzig: Engelmann.

Moll, L.C. (ed.) (1990), *Vygotsky and Education: Instructional Implications and Applications of Sociohistorical Psychology*. Cambridge: Cambridge University Press.

Münsterberg, H. (1920), *Psychology and the Teacher*. New York: D. Appleton and Company.

Odell, C.W. (1922), *The Use of Intelligence Tests as a Basis of School Organization and Instruction*. Urbana, IL: University of Illinois.

Odell, C.W. (1930), *Educational Measurement in High School*. New York: The Century Co.

Peterson, J. (1926/1969), *Early Conceptions and Tests of Intelligence*. Westport, CT: Greenwood Press.

Petrova, A. (1925). 'Deti-primitivy: Psikhogicheskij analiz', in M. Gurevich (ed.), *Voprosy Pedologii i Detskoj Psikhonevrologii*. Moscow: Zhizn' i Znanie, pp. 60–92.

Piaget, J. (1924), *Le Jugement at le Raisonnement chez l'Enfant*. Neuchatel: Delachaux et Niestlé.

Pinkus, B. (1988), *The Jews of the Soviet Union: The History of a National Minority*. Cambridge: Cambridge University Press.

Popenoe, H. (1927), 'A report of certain significant deficiencies of the accomplishment quotient'. *Journal of Educational Research*, 16, 40–7.

Potebnya, A.A. (1926/1989), 'Mysl i yazyk', in A.A. Potebnya, *Slovo i mif*. Moscow: Pravda, pp. 17–200.

Potebnya, A.A. (1989), *Slovo i mif*. Moscow: Izdatel'stvo Pravda.

Pratt, M.W., Kerig, P., Cowan, P.A., and Pape Cowan, C. (1999), 'Mothers and fathers teaching 3-year-olds: Authoritative parenting and adult scaffolding of young children's learning', in P. Lloyd and C. Fernyhough (eds), *Lev Vygotsky: Critical Assessments. Vol. 3. The Zone of Proximal Development*. London: Routledge, pp. 143–62.

Raeff, M. (1990). *Russia Abroad: A Cultural History of the Russian Emigration, 1919–1939*. Oxford: Oxford University Press.

Rahmani, L. (1973), *Soviet Psychology: Philosophical, Theoretical, and Experimental Issues*. New York: International Universities Press, Inc.

Razmyslov, P. (1934), 'O "kul'turno-istoricheskoy teorii psikhologii" Vygotskogo i Luriya'. *Kniga i Proletarskaya Revolyutsiya*, 4, 78–86.

Razmyslov, P. (1934/2000), 'On Vygotsky's and Luria's "cultural-historical theory of psychology"'. *Journal of Russian and East European Psychology*, 38, 45–58.

Reed, H.B. (1924), 'The effect of training on individual differences'. *Journal of Experimental Psychology*, 7, 186–200.

Rogoff, B. (1990), *Apprenticeship in Thinking: Cognitive Development in Social Contexts*. New York: Oxford University Press.

Rogoff, B. (2003), *The Cultural Nature of Human Development*. Oxford: Oxford University Press.

Rossolimo, G.J. (1926), *Das Psychologische Profil*. Halle: Marhold.

Rudik, P.A. (1932), 'Bourgeois influences in the psychological measurements of the intellect'. *Psikhologiya*, 3, 3–7.

Rudneva, E.I. (1937), *Pedologicheskie isvrashcheniya Vygotskogo*. Moscow: Gosudarstvennoe Uchebno-Pedagogicheskoe Izdatel'stvo.

Sacks, O. (1982), *Awakenings*. London: Picador.

Sacks, O. (1985), *The Man who Mistook his Wife for a Hat*. London: Picador.

Sacks, O. (1989), *Seeing Voices: A Journey into the World of the Deaf*. Berkeley, CA: University of California Press.

Sacks, O. (1995), *An Anthropologist on Mars: Seven Paradoxical Tales*. New York: Alfred A. Knopf.

Scarborough, H.S., and Parker, J.D. (2003), 'Matthew effects in children with learning disabilities: Development of reading, IQ, and psychosocial problems from grade 2 to grade 8'. *Annals of Dyslexia*, 53, 1–12.

Schaffer, H.R. (1984), *The Child's Entry into a Social World*. New York: Academic Press.

Schniermann, A.L. (1928), 'Present-day tendencies in Russian psychology'. *Journal of General Psychology*, 1, 397–404.

Scribner, S., and Cole, M. (1981), *The Psychology of Literacy*. Cambridge, MA: Harvard University Press.

Senelick, L. (1982), *Gordon Craig's Moscow Hamlet: A Reconstruction*. Westport, CT: Greenwood Press.

Shif, Z.I. (1935), *Razvitie nauchnykh ponyatiy u shkol'nika*. Moscow-Leningrad: Gosudarstvennoe Uchebno-Pedagogicheskoe Izdatel'stvo.

Shishov, A. (1928), 'Mal'chiki-uzbeki. Antropometricheskie issledovania'. *Meditsinskaya Mysl' Uzbekistana*, 4, 16–27.

Shpet, G.G. (1927/1989), 'Vvedenie v etnicheskuyu psikhologiyu', in G.G. Shpet, *Sochineniya*. Moscow: Pravda, pp. 475–574.

Shpet, G.G. (1989), *Sochineniya*. Moscow: Izdatel'stvo Pravda.

Shtilerman, A. (1928), 'Materialy psikhologicheskogo issledovania uzbekskikh shkol'nikov st. gor. Tashkenta po pereredaktirovannomu kratkomu Rossolimo'. *Meditsinskaya Mysl' Uzbekistana*, 4, 42–52.

Solov'ev, V.K. (1929), 'Godichnyy opyt ispytaniya obshchey odarennosti uzbekov i metodicheskiy analiz serii VSU RKKA'. *Psikhotekhnika is Psikhofiziologiya Truda*, 2–3, 151–67.

Stanovich, K.E. (1986), 'Matthew effects in reading: Some consequences of individual differences in the acquisition of literacy'. *Reading Research Quarterly*, 21, 360–407.

Stern, D.N. (1985), *The Interpersonal World of the Infant*. New York: Basic Books.

Stern, W. (1920), *Die Intelligenz der Kinder und Jugendlichen und die Methoden ihrer Untersuchung*. Leipzig: Barth.

Sternberg, R.J., and Grigorenko, E.L. (2002), *Dynamic Testing: The Nature and Measurement of Learning Potential*. Cambridge: Cambridge University Press.

Stevens, J.A. (1982). 'Children of the revolution: Soviet Russia's homeless children (bezprizorniki) in the 1920s'. *Russian History/Histoire Russe*, 9 (2–3), 242–64.

Strakhov, I.V. (1930), 'Against formalism in psychology'. *Psikhologiya*, 2, 145–87.

Talankin, A.A. (1931), 'O povorote na psikhologicheskom fronte'. *Sovetskaya Psikhonevrologiya*, 2–3, 8–23.

Terman, L.M. (1920), 'The use of intelligence tests in the grading of school children'. *Journal of Educational Research*, 1, 20–32.

Terman, L.M. (1921), *The Intelligence of School Children*. London: George G. Harrap & Co.

Terman, L.M., Dickson, V.E., Sutherland, A.H., Franzen, R.H., Tupper, C.R., and Fernald, G. (1923), *Intelligence Tests and School Reorganization*. Yonkers-on-Hudson, NY: World Book Company.

Thurnwald, R. (1922), 'Psychologie des primitiven Menschen', in G. Kafka (ed.), *Handbuch der vergleichenden Psychologie. Vol. I*. Munich: Verlag von Ernst Reinhardt, pp. 147–320.

Thurnwald, R. (1928), 'Varianten und Frühformen des Denkens und der Gestaltung: Prae-Logik?'. *Zeitschrift für Völkerpsychologie und Soziologie*, 4, 324–30.

Thurnwald, R. (1938), 'Der kulturelle Hintergrund primitiven Denkens', in H. Piéron and I. Meyerson (eds), *Onzième congrès international de psychologie*. Agen: Imprimerie Moderne, pp. 184–95.
Torgerson, T.L. (1922), 'The efficiency quotient as a measure of achievement'. *Journal of Educational Research*, 6, 25–32.
Torgerson, T.L. (1926), 'Is classification by mental ages and intelligence quotients worth while?'. *Journal of Educational Research*, 13 (3), 171–80.
Valsiner, J. (1988), *Developmental Psychology in the Soviet Union*. Brighton: Harvester Press.
Valsiner, J. (2000), *Culture and Human Development*. London: SAGE Publications.
Valsiner, J., and Van der Veer, R. (1993), 'The encoding of distance: The concept of the zone of proximal development and its interpretations', in R.R. Cocking and K.A. Renninger (eds), *The Development and Meaning of Psychological Distance*. Hillsdale, NJ: Erlbaum, pp. 35–62.
Valsiner, J., and Van der Veer, R. (2000), *The Social Mind: Construction of the Idea*. Cambridge: Cambridge University Press.
Van der Veer, R. (1994), 'The forbidden colors game: An argument in favor of internalization?', in R. Van der Veer, M.H. van IJzendoorn and J. Valsiner (eds), *Reconstructing the Mind: Replicability in Research on Human Development*. Norwood, NJ: Ablex Publishing Corporation, pp. 233–54.
Van der Veer, R. (1996a), 'The concept of culture in Vygotsky's thinking'. *Culture & Psychology*, 2, 247–63.
Van der Veer, R. (1996b), 'On some historical roots and present-day doubts: A reply to Nicolopoulou and Weintraub'. *Culture & Psychology*, 2, 457–63.
Van der Veer, R. (2000), 'Some reflections concerning Galperin's theory'. *Human Development*, 43, 99–102.
Van der Veer, R. (2003), 'Primitive mentality reconsidered'. *Culture & Psychology*, 9, 179–84.
Van der Veer, R. (2004), 'The making of a developmental psychologist', in J. Valsiner (ed.), *Heinz Werner and Developmental Science*. New York: Kluwer Academic Publishers, pp. 75–105.

Van der Veer, R. (2006), 'A radical approach to teaching and learning. Review of M. Hedegaard & S. Chaiklin, Radical-local teaching and learning'. *British Journal of Educational Studies*, 56, 265–7.

Van der Veer, R. (2007), 'Vygotsky in context: 1900–1935', in H. Daniels, M. Cole and J.V. Wertsch (eds), *The Cambridge Companion to Vygotsky*. New York: Cambridge University Press, pp. 21–49.

Van der Veer, R., and Valsiner, J. (1991), *Understanding Vygotsky: A Quest for Synthesis*. Oxford: Blackwell.

Van der Veer, R., and Valsiner, J. (1994), *The Vygotsky Reader*. Oxford: Blackwell.

Van der Veer, R., and Van Ijzendoorn, M.H. (1988), 'Early childhood attachment and later problem solving: A Vygotskian perspective', in J. Valsiner (ed.), *Child Development within Culturally Structured Environments: Parental and Adult-child Interaction. Vol. 1*. Norwood, NJ: Ablex Publishing Corporation, pp. 215–46.

Vedenov, A.A. (1932), 'Regarding the subject matter of psychology', *Psikhologiya*, 3, 43–58.

Vygodskaya, G.L., and Lifanova, T.M. (1996), *Lev Semenovich Vygotskiy: Zhizn, deyate'nost', shtrikhi k portretu*. Moscow: Smysl.

Vygotski, L.S. (1929), 'The problem of the cultural development of the child (II)'. *Pedagogical Seminary and Journal of Genetic Psychology*, 36, 415–34.

Vygotsky, L.S. (1916a). '"Peterburg" Andreya Belogo'. *Letopis'*, 12, 327–28.

Vygotsky, L.S. (1916b). 'Literaturnye zametki. "Peterburg". Roman Andreya Belogo'. *Novyj Put'*, 47, 27–32.

Vygotsky, L.S. (1917). 'Avodim Khoin'. *Novyj Put'*, 11–12, 8–10.

Vygotsky, L.S. (1923a). 'Evrejskij teatr. Sil'va. "A mensh zol men zajn"'. *Nash Ponedel'nik*, 30, 3.

Vygotsky, L.S. (1923b). 'Evrejskij teatr. Koldun'ya. "Dos ferblonzele sheifele"'. *Nash Ponedel'nik*, 33, 3.

Vygotsky, L.S. (1923c). 'Evrejskij teatr. Bar Kokhba. "Der eshiva bokher"'. *Nash Ponedel'nik*, 34, 3.

Vygotsky, L.S. (1923d). '10 dnej, kotorye potryasli mir'. *Polesskaya Pravda*, 1081, 23 December.

Vygotsky, L.S. (1925), 'Principles of social education for deaf and dumb children in Russia', in *International Conference on the Education of the Deaf*. London: William H. Taylor and Sons, pp. 227–37.

Vygotsky, L.S. (1925/1971), *The Psychology of Art*. Cambridge, MA: MIT Press.

Vygotsky, L.S. (1926). *Pedagogicheskaya Psikhologiya: Kratkij Kurs*. Moscow: Izdatel'stvo Rabotnik Prosveshcheniya.

Vygotsky, L.S. (1929a), 'K voprosu ob intellekte antropidov v svjazi s rabotami V. Kolera'. *Estvestvoznanie i Marksizm*, 2, 131–53.

Vygotsky, L.S. (1929b), 'K voprosu o plane nauchno-issledovatel'skoy raboty po pedologii natsional'nykh men'shinstv'. *Pedologiya*, 3, 367–77.

Vygotsky, L.S. (1929/1935), 'Predistoriya pis'mennoy rechi', in L.S. Vygotsky, *Umstvennoe razvitie detey v protsesse obucheniya*. Moscow-Leningrad: Uchpedgiz, pp. 73–95.

Vygotsky, L.S. (1930), 'Strukturnaya psikhologiya', in L. Vygotsky, S. Gellershteyn, B. Fingert and M. Shirvindt (eds), *Osnovnye techeniya sovremennoy psikhologii*. Moscow: Gosudarstvennoe Izdatel'stvo, pp. 84–125.

Vygotsky, L.S. (1930/1960), 'Povedenie zhivotnykh i cheloveka', in L.S. Vygotsky, *Razvitie Vysshikh Psikhicheskikh Funktsij*. Moscow: Izdatel'stvo Pedagogicheskikh Nauk, pp. 397–457.

Vygotsky, L.S. (1930/1997), 'On psychological systems', in R.W. Rieber and J. Wollock (eds), *The Collected Works of L.S. Vygotsky. Vol. 3. Problems of the Theory and History of Psychology*. New York: Plenum Press, pp. 91–107.

Vygotsky, L.S. (1931/1983). 'Istoriya razvitiya vysshikh psikhicheskikh funktsij', in L.S. Vygotsky, *Sobranie Sochinenij. Tom 3. Problemy Razvitijya Psikhiki*. Moscow: Pedagogika, pp. 5–328.

Vygotsky, L.S. (1933/1935a), 'Problema obucheniya i umstvennogo razvitiya v shkol'nom vozraste', in L.S. Vygotsky, *Umstvennoe razvitie detey v protsesse obucheniya*. Moscow-Leningrad: Uchpedgiz, pp. 3–19.

Vygotsky, L.S. (1933/1935b), 'Obuchenie i razvitie v shkol'nom vozraste', in L.S. Vygotsky, *Umstvennoe razvitie detey v protsesse obucheniya*. Moscow-Leningrad: Uchpedgiz, pp. 20–32.

Vygotsky, L.S. (1933/1935c), 'O pedologicheskom analize pedagogicheskogo protsessa', in L.S. Vygotsky, *Umstvennoe razvitie detey v protsesse obucheniya*. Moscow-Leningrad: Uchpedgiz, pp. 116–34.

Vygotsky, L.S. (1933/1935d), 'Razvitie zhiteyskikh i nauchnykh ponyatiy v shkol'nom vozraste', in L.S. Vygotsky, *Umstvennoe razvitie detey v protsesse obucheniya*. Moscow-Leningrad: Uchpedgiz, pp. 96–115.

Vygotsky, L.S. (1933/1935e), 'Dinamika umstvennogo razvitiya shkol'nika v svyazi s obucheniem', in L.S. Vygotsky, *Umstvennoe razvitie detey v protsesse obucheniya*. Moscow-Leningrad: Uchpedgiz, pp. 33–52.

Vygotsky, L.S. (1933/1966), 'Igra i ee rol' v psikhicheskom razvitii rebenka'. *Voprosy Psikhologii*, 6, 62–76.

Vygotsky, L.S. (1933/1984), 'Problema vozrasta', in L.S. Vygotsky, *Sobranie Sochinenyy. Tom 4. Detskaya Psikhologiya*. Moscow: Pedagogika, pp. 244–68.

Vygotsky, L.S. (1934a), *Myshlenie i rech: Psikhologicheskie issledovaniya*. Moscow: Gosudarstvennoe Sotsial'no-Ekonomicheskoe Izdatel'stvo.

Vygotsky, L.S. (1934b), 'Thought in schizophrenia'. *Archives of Neurology and Psychiatry*, 31, 1063–77.

Vygotsky, L.S. (1934/1977), 'Psychology and the theory of the localization of mental functions', in R.W. Rieber and J. Wollock (eds), *The Collected Works of L.S. Vygotsky. Vol. 3. Problems of the Theory and History of Psychology*. New York: Plenum Press, pp. 139–44.

Vygotsky, L.S. (1935), *Osnovy pedologii*. Leningrad: Izdanie Instituta.

Vygotsky, L.S. (1956), *Izbrannye Psikhologicheskie Issledovaniya*. Moscow: Izdatel'stvo APN RSFSR.

Vygotsky, L.S. (1960), *Razvitie Vysshikh Psikhicheskikh Funktsij*. Moscow: Izdatel'stvo APN RSFSR.

Vygotsky, L.S. (1982a), *Sobranie Sochineni. Tom Pervyj. Voprosy Teorii i Istorii Psikhologii*. Moscow: Pedagogika.

Vygotsky, L.S. (1982b), *Sobranie Sochineni. Tom Vtorojj. Problemy Obshchej Psikhologii*. Moscow: Pedagogika.

Vygotsky, L.S. (1983a), *Sobranie Sochineni. Tom Tretij. Problemy Razvitiya Psikhiki*. Moscow: Pedagogika.

Vygotsky, L.S. (1983b), *Sobranie Sochineni. Tom Chetvertyj. Detskaya Psikhologiya*. Moscow: Pedagogika.

Vygotsky, L.S. (1984a), *Sobranie Sochineni. Tom Pjatyj. Osnovy Defektologii*. Moscow: Pedagogika.
Vygotsky, L.S. (1984b), *Sobranie Sochineni. Tom Shestoj. Nauchnoe Nasledstvo*. Moscow: Pedagogika.
Vygotsky, L.S. (1962), *Thought and Language*. Cambridge, MA: MIT Press.
Vygotsky, L.S. (1965), 'Psychology and localization of functions'. *Neuropsychologia*, 3, 381–6.
Vygotsky, L.S. (1986), *Psikhologiya iskusstva* (3rd edn). Moscow: Iskusstvo.
Vygotsky, L.S. (1987), *Psikhologiya iskusstva*. Moscow: Pedagogika.
Vygotsky, L.S., and Luria, A.R. (1930a), 'The function and fate of egocentric speech', in *Ninth International Congress of Psychology. Proceedings and Papers. New Haven, September 1–7, 1929*. Princeton: Psychological Review Company, pp. 464–5.
Vygotsky, L.S., and Luria, A.R. (1930b), *Etyudy po Istorii Povedeniya: Obez'yana, Primitiv, Rebenok*. Moscow-Leningrad: Gosudarstvennoe Izdatel'stvo.
Vygotsky, L.S., and Luria, A.R. (1993), *Studies on the History of Behavior: Ape, Primitive, Child*. Hillsdale, NJ: Lawrence Erlbaum Associates.
Walberg, H.J., and Tsai, S. (1983), 'Matthew effects in education'. *American Educational Research Journal*, 20, 359–73.
Wells, F.L. (1927), *Mental Tests in Clinical Practice*. Yonkers-on Hudson, NY: World Book Company.
Wenger, E. (1998), *Communities of Practice: Learning, Meaning, and Identity*. New York: Cambridge University Press.
Werner, H. (1924), *Die Ursprünge der Lyrik: eine entwicklungspsychologische Untersuchung*. München: Reinhardt.
Werner, H. (1926), *Einführung in die Entwicklungspsychologie*. Leipzig: Barth.
Werner, H. (1931), 'Raum und Zeit in den Urformen der Künste'. *Zeitschrift für Aesthetik und allgemeine Kunstwissenschaft. Beiheft*, 25, 68–86.
Wertsch, J.V. (1981), 'Adult-child interaction as a source of self-regulation in children', in S.R. Yussen (ed.), *The Development of Reflection*. New York: Academic Press.
Wertsch, J.V. (1985), *Vygotsky and the Social Formation of Mind*. Cambridge, MA: Harvard University Press.

Wilson, F.T. (1926), 'Some achievements of pupils of the same mental ages but different intelligence quotients'. *Journal of Educational Research*, 14, 43–53.

Wilson, W.R. (1928), 'The misleading accomplishment quotient'. *Journal of Educational Research*, 17, 1–10.

Wood, D. (1980), 'Teaching the young child: Some relationships between social interaction, language and thought', in D.R. Olson (ed.), *The Social Foundations of Language and Thought*. New York: Norton, pp. 280–96.

Wood, D., Bruner, J.S., and Ross, G. (1976), 'The role of tutoring in problem solving'. *Journal of Child Psychology and Psychiatry*, 17, 89–100.

Wood, D., Wood, H., and Middleton, D. (1978), 'An experimental evaluation of four face-to-face strategies'. *International Journal of Behavioral Development*, 1, 131–47.

Wozniak, R.H. (1999), 'Verbal regulation of motor behavior: Soviet research and non-Soviet replications', in P. Lloyd and C. Fernyhough (eds), *Lev Vygotsky: Critical Assessments. Vol. 2. Thought and Language*. London: Routledge, pp. 123–67.

Wygotski, L.S. (1929), 'Die genetischen Wurzeln des Denkens und der Sprache'. *Unter dem Banner des Marxismus*, 3, 450–70.

Yaroshevsky, M.G. (1987), 'Posleslovie', in L.S. Vygotsky, *Psikhologiya iskusstva*. Moscow: Pedagogika, pp. 292–323.

Yaroshevsky, M.G. (1989), *Lev Vygotsky*. Moscow: Progress Publishers.

Yaroshevsky, M.G. (1993), *L.S. Vygotsky: V poiskakh novoy psikhologii*. St. Peterburg: Izdatel'stvo Fonda Istorii Nauki.

Yerkes, R.M. (1916), *The Mental Life of Monkeys and Apes*. New York: Holt.

Yerkes, R.M. (1925), *Almost Human*. New York: Century.

Yerkes, R.M., and Learned, E.W. (1925), *Chimpanzee Intelligence and its Vocal Expression*. Baltimore: Williams & Wilkins Company.

Yerkes, R.M., and Yerkes, A.W. (1929), *The Great Apes: A Study of Anthropoid Life*. New Haven: Yale University Press.

Zaporozhets, A.V. (1930), 'Umstvennoe razvitie i psikhicheskie osobennosti oyrotskikh detey'. *Pedologiya*, 2, 222–35.

Zivin, G. (ed.) (1979), *The Development of Self-Regulation Through Private Speech*. New York: John Wiley.

Name Index

Abel'skaya, 28
Ageyev, 97
Aikhenvald, 28, 36, 106
Ainsworth, 116
Akhmatova, 20
Arievitch, 119
Ashpiz, 14

Babel, 20
Badley, 136
Balamore, 63
Barash, 108
Basov, 2, 77
Bauer, 77, 138
Beba, 14
Bekhterev, 2, 14, 42, 47
Belyj, 20
Benjamin, 1
Berdyaev, 38
Binet, 75, 77–8, 85, 98, 130
Bishop, 76
Blok, 20
Blonsky, 2, 17, 46, 77, 137–8
Boring, 3–5, 75
Borovski, 2
Brill, 1
Brooks, 76
Brown, 127–9
Bruner, 4, 114–5
Budoff, 129–30, 132

Bulanov, 98
Bulgakov, 20
Bunin, 20, 40, 106
Burks, 76
Burt, 57, 75, 78–9
Butterworth, 116

Campione, 127–9
Catherine, 29
Chagall, 20
Chaiklin, 78, 119–21
Chamberlain, 28, 106
Chekhov, 106
Chelpanov, 17, 22, 77
Cole, 4–6, 64, 110, 122–24
Coy, 76
Craig, 36
Crusoe, 4

Daniels, 6, 119
Darwin, 42–3
Davydov, 120
De Waal, 108
Dewey, 136–7
Droogleever Fortuyn, 138
Dunn, 116

Efimov, 98
Ehrenburg, 20
Eikhenbaum, 39

Eisenstein, 20–1, 31
El'konin, 113, 120
El-Lissitzky, 20
Engels, 19, 22, 28–9, 54
Esenin, 20
Evans-Pritchard, 55

Feigenberg, 14–5
Feofanov, 28
Fernyhough, 8
Feuerstein, 87, 130–3
Fordyce, 76
Frank, 28

Gal'perin, 117–9, 121, 131, 133
Gilbert, 15
Goddard, 75
Golod, 140
Gornfeld, 36
Gould, 57, 75
Grigorenko, 127–8, 130, 132
Grover, 116

Haenen, 118–9
Haggbloom, 3
Hahnemann, 38
Hall, 1
Hanfmann, 2
Hedegaard, 119–21
Henmon, 109
Hines, 75

Ivanov, 38

Jahoda, 55
James, 30, 89, 107
Janet, 4, 30
Joravsky, 77

Kafka, 29
Kallom, 76
Kandinsky, 20
Kasanin, 2
Kaye, 116
Kerschensteiner, 136
Khodasevich, 20
Koffka, 2, 89–90
Köhler, 54
Kornilov, 2, 22, 77, 107
Kozulin, 4, 6, 15, 116, 119, 123, 131, 137–8
Kozyrev, 28
Krupskaya, 19, 24, 77, 137–8
Krylov, 39
Kurek, 77, 98, 110

Lange, 77
Lashley, 47, 69
Lave, 110, 124–6
Learned, 54
Lenin, 19, 22, 29, 138
Leontiev, 1, 58–9, 113, 117–8
Leroy, 55, 122
Lévy-Bruhl, 51, 55–6, 125
Lewin, 2
Leyland, 116
Lifanova, 13–4, 17, 25, 31
Light, 116
Lloyd, 8
Lunacharsky, 19
Luria, A.R., 1–2, 4, 8, 21, 24, 27–8, 31, 66, 71–3, 97–106, 113, 117, 121–3, 139–40
Luria, E.A., 26

Malevich, 20
Mandel'shtam, 20, 28

Marx, 19, 22, 29, 43–4, 54
Mateer, 76
Mayakovsky, 20
McCarthy, 79
McCrory, 76
McLeish, 27
McNaughton, 116
Medvedev, 110
Meins, 116
Melk-Koch, 57
Merton, 109
Meumann, 79
Meyerhold, 20
Middleton, 115
Moll, 6, 119
Montessori, 136, 138
Münsterberg, 47

Nabokov, 20, 106
Nechaev, 77
Neopikhonova, 28

Odell, 87
Owell, 79

Parkhurst, 136
Pasternak, 20
Paustovsky, 20
Pavlov, 2, 14, 42–5, 47, 89, 107
Petersen, 136
Peterson, 75
Petrova, 51, 57, 100, 102, 128
Piaget, 2–3, 7, 63, 88, 90, 92, 140
Pinkus, 15
Platonov, 20
Plekhanov, 42
Popenoe, 76
Potebnya, 39, 52–3

Pratt, 116
Prokofiev, 20

Rahmani, 77, 119
Razmyslov, 28, 105–6
Reed, H.B, 109
Reed, J., 30
Remizov, 20
Rogoff, 124–6
Ross, 115
Rossolimo, 77, 98
Rozanov, 38
Rudik, 77
Rudneva, 29

Sacks, 8, 49, 70–1, 108–9
Schaffer, 116
Schniermann, 2
Schubert, 139
Scribner, 6, 122–4
Senelick, 36
Shakespeare, 14, 17, 35–7, 40
Sherrington, 42
Shif, 92–4
Shishov, 98
Shklovsky, 39, 106
Shochet, 132
Sholokhov, 20
Shostakovich, 20
Shpet, 17, 39, 52–3
Shtilerman, 98, 110
Simon, 75, 98
Solov'ev, 98
Spinoza, 30
Stalin, 27, 29
Stanislavsky, 20, 36, 106
Stanovich, 109
Starch, 109

Steiner, 38, 136
Stern, D.N., 116
Stern, W., 75, 79
Sternberg, 127–8, 130, 132
Stetsenko, 119
Stevens, 18
Stravinsky, 20
Sutton, 4

Tairov, 20
Terman, 57, 75–6, 78–9
Thurnwald, 51, 55–7
Thurstone, 75
Tolstoy, 106, 135
Torgerson, 76, 109
Trotsky, 27, 42
Tsai, 109
Tsvetaeva, 20
Turko, 28
Tynyanov, 39

Valsiner, 2–3, 5, 8, 16, 19, 21–2, 26, 28, 31, 38, 56, 94, 98–100, 110, 134
Van der Veer, 2, 4–5, 8, 16, 19, 21–2, 26, 28, 30–1, 38, 52, 55–6, 58, 68, 94, 98–100, 110, 116, 119, 121

Van IJzendoorn, 116
Vedenov, 28
Von Humboldt, 53
Vygodskaya, C.M., 13
Vygodskaya, G.L., 13–4, 17, 25, 31
Vygodsky, D., 13, 28
Vygodsky, L.S., 13, 29
Vygodsky, S.L., 13

Washoe, 4
Watson, 2, 14, 47
Wells, 75
Wenger, 124, 126
Werner, 55–6, 67–8
Wertsch, 7, 61
Wilson, 76
Wood, 114–6, 128–9
Wozniak, 63
Wygotski, 1

Yakobson, 39
Yaroshevsky, 36–7
Yerkes, 5, 54, 57, 75

Zalkind, 77
Zamyatin, 20
Zaporozhets, 98, 113
Zivin, 8

Subject Index

aborigines, 56–7
abstract reductionism, 23; thinking, 51–2
acculturation, 134
achievement quotient, 76; score, 76
actual development, 81–2
aesthetic reaction, 39
afterlife, 37
annus terribilis, 18
anti-Semitism, 15–6
Arbeitsschule, 136
arithmetic, 60, 91, 123–4
Art Theater, 20
attachment theory, 116

Battleship Potemkin, 20
behaviorism, 3
bezprizorniki, 18
bourgeois, 22, 27, 42, 44, 77
Braille script, 48, 67
brain, 8, 23, 64–5, 67–74, 109; centers, 68–9, 73; lesion, 8, 72; system, 69–70, 72, 74
Bushmen, 56

catharsis, 39, 41
Central Committee, 29
Chamber Theater, 20
Chuvash, 98

classical conditioning, 43, 89
classification, 53, 99–100, 102, 129, 135
clinical psychology, 24, 38
cognition, 88, 91–2, 117, 124–5
cognitive development, 7, 66, 84, 88–9, 92, 95–6, 114, 117, 123, 126, 133–4
collectivization, 110
colored cards, 58–60, 84
communicative speech, 7
compensation, 50, 70, 73–4
concentration camps, 28
conditional reflexes, 43–5
conscious realization, 90, 133
consciousness, 44, 47, 53, 105
Cro Magnon man, 108
cross-cultural, 98, 126
cultural deprivation, 6, 129, 133; development, 1, 52, 56, 83; psychology, 5, 53, 135; tool, 6–8, 28, 41, 48–9, 51–2, 57–61, 63–4, 67, 73–4, 84, 95, 97–8, 100, 104, 117, 126, 133–4
cultural-historical theory, 4–5, 45, 48, 52–3, 63, 74, 104, 122, 139

Dalton plan, 136; school, 46
dancing tables, 38

deaf-mute, 52, 64, 107
decimal system, 60
defectology, 8, 24
dekulakization, 110
disabled children, 8, 128–9
disadvantaged children, 64, 129
discharge, 41
doctoral dissertation, 14, 38–9
doubled experience, 44–5
dual testing procedure, 6, 83, 96, 126
dynamic assessment, 6, 119, 126–8, 134–5

educational system, 42, 44, 77–8, 87, 95, 97, 120–1, 130, 137–8
egocentric speech, 1–2, 7, 62–3, 119
engram, 69
enrichment programs, 6, 133–4
ethnic background, 15–6, 27, 95, 97
ethnocentrism, 57
ethnopsychology, 53
eugenics, 57, 75, 77
everyday concepts, 92, 95, 126; knowledge, 120; thinking, 96, 125–6
evolution, 43, 65, 120
external mediation, 64, 72, 119; sign, 60, 71–2

fable, 39, 40–1
feeble-minded, 50–2, 57, 108, 128–9
forbidden colors, 58, 62, 84, 118
forensic psychology, 28

formal discipline, 91
formalist schools, 39
formats, 115

gainers, 129, 132–3
gentle breath, 40
Gestalt, 89
graduated-prompts, 127
guided participation, 125–6
Gulag Archipelago, 29

Hamlet, 14, 17, 35–8, 40–1
handicapped children, 24, 49–50, 52, 64
hereafter, 42
heuristics, 89, 131
higher psychological functions, 52–3, 123
historical experience, 44–6
holocaust, 130
hypnosis, 38

illiteracy, 106
Indians, 56
industrial psychology, 28
innate intelligence, 75; reflexes, 43–4
inner speech, 7, 62, 90–1, 118–9
instruction, 6, 76, 78–80, 82, 84–92, 94–7, 99, 104, 115, 119, 123–8, 133–4, 136
intelligence, 57, 75–6, 79, 82, 88, 126, 130; tests, 57, 75, 79, 107
intelligentsia, 77
internal mediation, 59, 64, 119
internalization, 117
interpsychological, 83, 116

intrapsychological, 83, 116
IQ tests, 6, 75–78, 87, 98–9, 128–30
Islamic culture, 56

Jena Plan, 136
Jews, 13–6, 18–9, 27, 30, 130

kolkhoz, 99–100, 105–6
kulak, 99

labor school, 1, 46, 136–7
language, 7–8, 35, 39, 49–50, 53–5, 60–1, 63–4, 66–8, 70–1, 73, 91, 102, 122–3, 126
learning by doing, 137
learning potential, 82, 126–8
leveling effect, 79, 84, 86–7
literacy, 49, 52, 97, 100, 104, 121–4, 126, 133–4

madrassah, 122–3
manipulation, 118–9, 121
Marxism, 1, 17, 19, 22, 28–9, 38, 52–4, 139
mastery, 90–2, 133
Matthew effect, 86, 109
maturation, 64, 67–8, 73, 88–90
mediation, 64, 114
mediator, 130–1
mental age, 76, 79–81, 83; disabilities, 8; level, 87; tests, 75–7, 78, 82–3, 87, 95, 98, 131
mentally retarded, 48, 50, 129
metacognitive skills, 131
method acting, 106
minority groups, 50, 52, 77, 105

mismatch, 48–9, 52
models, 120–1, 134
modifiable, 133
monotheism, 56
'Moslem influence', 106

nationalism, 97, 105
Nobel Prize, 20, 40
nongainers, 129, 132–3
nonmodifiable, 133

occipital lobe, 69
October Revolution, 16, 18–9, 30, 38, 43, 45
ontogeny, 59, 60–1, 65, 67, 72
oral speech, 50, 90–1
organically impaired, 133
osoznanie, 90–1, 133
other-regulation, 61, 115
ovladenie, 90–1, 133
Oyrot, 98

Pale of settlement, 15, 29
Parkinson's disease, 71, 73
Party, 19, 22, 26–30, 77, 105, 138; decree, 28–9
pedology, 28, 81, 138; decree, 78, 113
PhD, 38
phrenologists, 70
physical handicaps, 8
pneumograph, 106
pneumothorax, 30
pogroms, 15
polytechnic school, 46, 140
polytheism, 56
possible development, 81

Press Museum, 21
pretend play, 110
preverbal thought, 62
priem, 39
primitive thought, 51–2, 54–8, 65, 100, 125, 128–9; society, 55–6
prise de conscience, 90
production relations, 28
prognosis, 51, 78, 82, 84, 128
progressive schools, 137
progressivism, 138
psychoanalysis, 28
psycholinguistics, 7
psychological expedition, 1
psychoneurology, 8

racist, 57
reaction apparatus, 47
reactions, 44–5, 47, 65, 77, 107
reactology, 28
rearmament, 66
reasoning, 6, 67, 94–5, 104
Red Army, 20
reflection, 54, 91–2, 95, 122
reflexes, 42, 44, 64–5, 72, 107
reflexology, 28
regression, 72–3, 109, 132
rehabilitation, 24
relativity theory, 21

Sahara, 44, 46
scaffolding, 114, 134, 140
schooling, 56–7, 74, 79, 98, 100, 102–4, 122, 124, 126, 133
scientific concepts, 6, 88, 92, 94–5, 97, 100, 114, 119, 131, 134
self-regulation, 61, 83, 115

semantic field, 62
semiotics, 53
sensitive period, 138
sensitivity, 15, 134
shamanism, 56
Shanyavsky University, 14, 17, 21, 106
short circuit, 39
short story, 39–41
sign language, 4, 49–50, 107
signs, 48, 53, 57, 60, 121
social experience, 44–5; other, 126, 134; psychology, 28; realism, 20; speech, 7, 62
sociogenetic law, 83–4
Soviet man, 41, 46, 97; period, 86; regime, 77, 97, 114; society, 5, 19; Union, 24, 42, 57, 75–8, 97–8, 137–8
speech, 1, 7, 15, 28, 49–50, 52–3, 60–4, 67, 73–4, 90–1, 118, 123
spiritism, 56
spoken language, 4
spontaneous concepts, 88, 92
stepwise formation of mental acts, 117–9
stoicism, 26
subordination, 72
syllogism, 51, 99, 131
systemic relationships, 69

tools, 49, 51–2, 54, 57–9, 63–4, 67, 74, 84, 97, 100, 121, 123, 134
tool-use, 54
tragedy, 35, 37, 39–41
transfer of learning, 110, 119, 124, 127–9

Tsarist Russia, 13, 15, 18; schools, 42
tuberculosis, 19, 23, 25–6, 29, 38
Tungus, 98

Uzbekistan, 28, 56, 98–9, 103, 105–6, 122
Uzbeks, 28, 56, 98

Vai, 122–3
verbalization, 121

visual illusions, 99
vocal speech, 1, 49
vulgar materialism, 23

Waldorf schools, 136
World War I, 19
written speech, 90

Zeitgeist, 3, 5, 38
zone of proximal development, 75, 78–9, 81–8, 94–96, 114, 116, 126, 138, 141

Lightning Source UK Ltd.
Milton Keynes UK
UKHW020624290421
382820UK00005B/95